MEMO joggers

Memory Tips for Math

Memorization and Learning Styles:
The Successful Way to Teach K-5 Math

By Donnalyn Yates, M.Ed

Published by:
Memory Joggers
www.memoryjoggers.com
info@memoryjoggers.com
Phone: 949-371-6760

Dedicated to my daughter Lise,

my best friend, encourager

and inspiration.

Word from the Author

Do you know how to teach children to memorize? If you are like most teachers and parents, probably not. In college we were never given any tools on the basics of memorization. It was assumed if we did a good job teaching the concept of math, students would naturally remember all of the information. Not so!!

In my first year of teaching, I used hands-on methods along with textbooks for teaching math, and I felt I did a good job. But at the end of the year I still had students counting on their fingers and forgetting what a lot of the math vocabulary meant. Since I had used successful memory techniques in college, I wondered if I could teach these same memory principles to children.

After several summers I developed a card system, using pictures, rhymes and stories to teach multiplication and division. The following school year, all of my students knew their multiplication and division facts after only 3 months. My peers wanted to know how I accomplished this, so I began copying my set of cards for them. Overnight I had a business called Memory Joggers. By speaking at teacher conventions I continued to get the word out.

By doing brain-based research on memory and learning styles, I developed even more material, which proved successful in the classroom. The students were having fun learning and remembering, plus all of the NCTM standards were met!

Memory Tips for Math is a compilation of many of these successful methods. Based on the "Multiple Intelligence" theory, I discovered many children are not Logical/Mathematical learners and they are the ones struggling with math. Their learning style is different and needs to be addressed. Learning challenged students make amazing progress using these memory tips.

After reading and using this book, I challenge you to find other memorization techniques on your own. Share them with me and together we can help all children succeed!

Donnalyn Yates

Introduction

Memory Tips for Math is a book for you, the teacher and parent, who want to help your students succeed in school and meet the NCTM standards. In this book you will learn how the brain retains information and specific memory techniques to use for different learning styles.

The three most common perceptual learning styles are visual learners (those who learn through seeing), auditory learners (those who learn through listening and verbalizing) and kinesthetic/tactile learners (those who learn by moving, doing and touching). Memorization is enhanced when you identify the learning style of a child and match it with a particular memory technique. It's easy and fun, as you will find out in the book!

Math vocabulary is confusing. Low test scores affirm this. Often times the student knows the procedure for solving a problem but doesn't understand the term used in the test question. You'll find that *Memory Tips for Math* is full of creative ideas for remembering vocabulary and math procedures. Children with learning disorders especially respond to these unique memory tips.

Memory Tips for Math uses rhymes, stories, pictures and associations to connect the information to the meaning. The sillier it is, the easier it is to remember! Turn on the right side of your brain and have fun! Your students certainly will.

Contents

Fractions Can Be Fun!

Deciphering Decimals

Geometry- Now this is Fun!

Geometry We Can Touch

The Why's and How's of Memory

Memory and the Educational System

Traditionally, the educational system has not been structured to adapt to the way the brain works. Most of the time we present material without considering how each child's brain learns and retains information. Over the past few years, substantial research has been conducted, proving brain-based education needs to be a critical basis for education. Renate and Geoffrey Caine in *Making Connections*, state that, "Understanding how the brain learns has implications for instructional design, administration, evaluation, the role of the school in the community, teachers' education, and a host of other issues related to educational reform. Brain-based learning is not a separate thrust or movement in education; it is an approach from which all education can benefit."

Memory is the mother of all wisdom
Aeschylus (circa 490 B.C.)

Brain-based education means understanding how the five senses help to improve memory. Neural research proves that we have natural built-in memory sites throughout the brain. These sites are connected to the five senses, giving each person visual, auditory, kinesthetic, olfaction and taste memories. People inherit different levels of ability in each area. If a person has strong auditory memory, information presented audibly will be more easily retained. If their visual memory is a stronger influence, they will learn better with pictures and drawings and things they can see. This is known as individual "Learning Styles".

The Three Structural Parts of Memory

The brain has three types of memory: **sensory** memory, **short-term** memory and **long-term** memory.

1. The sensory register receives information from the five senses: visual (seeing), auditory (hearing), kinesthetic or tactile (touching), olfactory (smell) and taste memory. It briefly registers the contact, but if nothing is done to make it an important event, the memory quickly fades. If you walked into a room, looked around and noticed the general layout of the room, smelled the coffee brewing and touched the chair but realized you were in the wrong room and quickly left, your sensory memory would register what you sensed but the information would probably not be retained unless something of significance happened.

2. The short term memory or working memory is used in our daily life for specific tasks. A routine task is performed such as eating, traveling, doing school assignments or working. Once the activity is ended, and if nothing of significance has happened, or there doesn't seem to be a need for the information, the memory associated with it begins to fade. It can be likened to an "in-basket" where information that is not needed is routinely dumped.

3. The long-term memory is the portion of the brain where memory is retained. Think of it as a filing cabinet where information is stored and can be easily retrieved. In order for information to be stored, a conscious effort or a repeated use of strategies is necessary. Emotional or traumatic situations are stored for use as a protective device for our well-being. If something is unique and strange it is often times remembered. As a parent and teacher, it is our goal to have as much information as possible retained in the child's long-term memory; therefore we need strategies and understanding to perform that function.

Strategies for Placing Information into Long Term Memory

There are a number of different ways information is moved from short-term memory into long term. Each child has different learning styles and what works with one person may not be relevant with another. Therefore it is necessary to try to explore all the methods of learning in order to meet each child's needs. Information is usually retained using three or four of these strategies.

1. Meaningfulness - It has to make sense. If the information is meaningful to the learner then it is easier to retain. A child cannot be told to remember that 2 plus 2 equals 4 until they are taught in concrete ways what adding means in relation to numbers. This is the method of teaching most widely used. Then why isn't it working? Meaningfulness is only one part of the puzzle. There are other parts needed to place information into long-term memory.

2. Familiarity - The more you know about a subject, the easier it is to learn new information about it. Learning builds upon learning. Again, we as teachers use this method. We teach addition, and then multiplication builds on the idea of repetitive addition.

If we teach a word problem about baseball to a child who is very sports minded, the problem will be more understandable. The child is relating the problem to perhaps an experience he or she had at a ball game. So familiarity with a subject prepares the way for placement into long-term memory.

3. Rhymes - This is a highly effective learning tool. Simple rhymes help us remember information. People who learned the rhyme, "In fourteen hundred and ninety-two, Columbus sailed the ocean blue," have that date impressed in their long-term memory.

Rhymes, like music, are easily remembered. The brain recognizes the similarities and the repeating sound and encodes the words easily. There is a sense of pleasure with rhyming which adds to the brain's ability to remember the information. "When it's fun, it's easily done!" That phrase is easy to remember. Now try remembering the same idea but with no rhyme. "When it is a fun activity it is easier to remember the information." As you can see, rhyming is a powerful tool!

4. Patterns - Finding a pattern, rule or underlying principle in the material enhances the memory process. For example, Mr. Leon Fleisher was an internationally famous pianist. Mr. Fleisher learned whole piano concerts of 20,000 distinct notes. He did this by finding underlying patterns in the music. Successful dancers memorize dance routines by finding the repeating pattern. Patterns exist in math and discovering these patterns helps the memory process.

5. Associations - It is easy to remember the outline of Italy because it looks like a boot. This illustrates the use of association. Association refers to relating what you want to learn to something you already know. Using association methods is one of the best retention mechanisms that can be employed in learning. It is also a method that is not used to it's maximum potential. Using mnemonics and word associations give the child a tool to help them remember.

6. Visualization - A very observant student once said, "If you don't know what a butterfly wing is and how it's made, you can draw it and then you'll know." That child was using the process of visualization to place the information into long-term memory.

Words that evoke images are coded dually in both the verbal and visual memory so that there is twice as great a likelihood of remembering them. Some children need to be taught how to visualize although others use this memory technique almost exclusively. Visual learners often struggle with math because they are not able to picture the concept. This book addresses these learners specifically.

7. Repetition - The more times a fact is repeated <u>aloud</u>, the more likely it will be remembered. Children need to hear themselves say the information in order for it to be remembered. Repetition along with bodily movement, and in rhyme format, is a very successful method. Repeating information within 24 hours is an important element.

8. Fun!!! - It is a proven fact that activities that are enjoyable are more easily stored in long-term memory. The brain will store pleasurable events for future use and discard boring ones. If a child's interest is sparked, learning will easily take place. The child is eager to repeat the activity over and over.

"Memory is greatly enhanced by association, repetition, understanding of meanings, rhyme and rhythm. Early folk ballads were sung in rhythm so that they could easily be remembered and re-sung by people who had not yet developed learning skills."

Hermann Ebbinghaus
Philosophy Professor and Memory Pioneer

What are Mnemonics?
Mnemonics (pronounced "new-mon-ics") are methods, devices, or even mental tricks for improving memory. The use of all mnemonic techniques requires that the items to be remembered be organized in personally meaningful and concrete ways. In other words, mnemonics are memory tips that form a mental picture.

Peg System
One mnemonic device is called the **Peg System**. In this system, items that are to be learned are hooked by vivid mental images onto the "pegs" that have already been learned in a certain order. This system is especially useful when something is to be learned in order or in steps.

Here is a list of peg words from one to ten. Other rhyming words can be used in place of those listed.

> One is a bun
> Two is a shoe
> Three is a tree
> Four is a door
> Five is a hive
> Six is sticks
> Seven is heaven
> Eight is a gate
> Nine is a vine
> Ten is a hen

All the peg words are concrete nouns that can easily be associated mentally with the items to be learned. This technique works by helping to build up pictures in the mind, in which the numbers are represented by things that rhyme with the number, and are linked to images that represent the things to be remembered. This method has been successfully used to teach multiplication and division as explained later in the book.

Acronyms

A second memory device is the use of **ACRONYMS**.   There are two steps involved in using this memory device.

1. Write down the first letter of each word after arranging the words in the order to be remembered.

2. Choose words that start with the same letters and also seem to go together to form a memorable sentence or phrase.

Example: Name the planets in their order from the sun, omitting poor Pluto!

<u>M</u>y <u>V</u>ery <u>E</u>xcellent <u>M</u>om <u>J</u>ust <u>S</u>erved <u>U</u>s <u>N</u>achos
(Mercury, Venus, Earth, Mars, Jupiter, Saturn, Uranus, Neptune.)

How do you spell arithmetic?

<u>A</u> <u>R</u>at <u>I</u>n <u>T</u>he <u>H</u>ouse <u>M</u>ight <u>E</u>at <u>T</u>he <u>I</u>ce <u>C</u>ream

The first letter in each word of this silly saying will spell "arithmetic". A picture can be added to help with the visualization process.

There are certain limitations to the use of acronyms. If a list is too long it will be difficult to make a meaningful sentence.

Learning Styles and Memorization

When teachers direct their curriculum to meet the needs of students' different learning styles, the results are amazing! Individuals have different sensory "pathways" that are specific to them. When information enters that "pathway" it is retained in short-term memory, but with repeated exposure and specific memory techniques it quickly moves into long-term memory.

The perceptual styles theory is based upon research that was conducted from 1975 to 1981 by Drs. Russell French, Daryl Gilley, and Ed Cherry. Since that time studies have been continued throughout the United States by researchers interested in the improvement of learning and teaching. Three of the most common learning modalities are visual learners, audio learners and kinesthetic learners.

Visual Learners
Learn through Seeing....
These learners need to see the teacher's body language and facial expression to fully understand the content of a lesson. They tend to prefer sitting at the front of the classroom to avoid visual obstructions (e.g. people's heads). They may think in pictures and learn best from visual displays including: diagrams, illustrated textbooks, overhead transparencies, videos, flip charts and handouts. During a lecture or classroom discussion, visual learners often prefer to take detailed notes to absorb the information.

Visual learners make up 65% of the population.
Characteristics of visual learners:
Use lists or outlines to organize thoughts
Remembers where information is located on a page
Sees pictures or words in the "mind's eye"
Has a vivid imagination
Becomes impatient or drifts away when extensive listening is required
Likes to do artwork
Likes to piece things together
Fond of doodling
Enjoys tracing words and pictures
Uses mnemonic methods to aid memory

Auditory/Verbal Learners
Learn through listening and speaking...
They learn best through verbal lectures, discussions, talking things through and listening to what others have to say. Auditory learners interpret the underlying meanings of speech through listening to tone of voice, pitch, speed and other nuances. Written information may have little meaning until it is heard. These learners often benefit from reading text aloud and using a tape recorder.

Auditory learners make up 30% of the population.
Characteristics of auditory learners:
Tends to remember and repeat ideas that are verbally presented
 Learns well through lectures
Is an excellent listener
Can reproduce symbols, letters or words by hearing them
Likes to talk
Enjoys plays
Can learn concepts by listening to tapes
Enjoys music
Enjoys question/answer sessions
Sets information to rhyme, rhythm, or music to aid retention
Finds small group discussions stimulating and informative
Must say facts/formulas/information over and over to retain

Kinesthetic/Tactile Learners
Learn through, moving, doing and touching...
Kinesthetic/tactile persons learn best through a hands-on approach, actively exploring the physical world around them. They may find it hard to sit still for long periods and often become distracted by their need for activity and exploration. These students have high energy levels. They think and learn best while moving. They often lose much of what is said during a lecture and have problems concentrating when asked to sit and read. These students prefer to do, rather than watch or listen.

Kinesthetic/tactile learners make up 5% of the population.

Characteristics of kinesthetic/tactile learners:
Learns by doing, direct involvement

Often fidgets or finds reasons to move

Is not very attentive to visual or auditory presentations

Wants to be "doing" something

Tries things out

Likes to manipulate objects

Gestures when speaking

Is often a poor listener

Responds to music by physical movement

Often finds success in physical response activities

Likes to move hands (doodling, tapping,) while learning

Knowing a student's learning style is important. Teachers and parents are able to respond to individual needs in a more appropriate manner. Frustration declines and self-esteem increases. Naturally students are happier because they feel accepted for who they are. They don't have to learn like someone else. They have special abilities. They are unique!

The secret of education is respecting the pupil.
Ralph Waldo Emerson

One, Two, Buckle my Shoe

Counting Rhymes to Ten - Let's Make a Book!

Rhymes are a very effective method for teaching children new ideas. Any time we can combine rhyming, pictures, writing and coloring, the brain is able to remember and store the information much easier. Plus, all children love making their very own books!

This counting rhyme from one to ten is fun for children to say aloud and can be quickly memorized. Reproducible pages are found in **Appendix A**, (pages 102 - 112.) Instruct the children to practice writing the number on the lines provided and color the picture. Add a colorful cover and the book is complete. Since rhymes are easy to remember, reading the rhymes aloud from their own book, aids the reading process too.

Counting to Ten

Run, **One**! Run for fun!
Can't you see, you're number **One**!

Two, two, shoes for you
Count them again, One, **two.**

Three, Three, Three, what do you see?
Three little birdies in the tree.
One, two, **three.**

Four, four, four. Four balls bouncing on the floor.
One, two, three, **four**

Five, five, take a dive
See five divers deep-sea dive!
One, two, three, four, **five**

Six chicks do some tricks.
How many chicks?
One, two, three, four, five, **six!**

Seven, seven. We count to **seven**
One, two, three, four, five, six, **seven!**

Eight, Eight. can't be late
To eat eight cookies off the plate!
One, two, three, four, five, six, seven, **eight**.

Nine, nine, Valentines
Some are yours and some are mine!
One, two, three, four, five, six, seven, eight, **nine**.

Ten, ten, Mother hen
Laid ten eggs in her pen.
One, two, three, four, five,
Six, seven, eight, nine, **ten**.

Counting to Twenty Rhyming Book

Try this old favorite for counting to twenty. Clapping while saying the rhyme adds fun and more rhythm. Children learn more rapidly when they visualize the pictures for each line. See **Appendix B**, (pages 113 – 123.) in the back of this book for reproducible masters. The student can write each line of the rhyme and color the picture. Add a color cover and the book is complete.

Counting Rhyme to Twenty
One, two, buckle my shoe.
Three, four, close the door.
Five, six, pick up sticks.
Seven, eight, lay them straight.
Nine, ten, a big fat hen.
Eleven, twelve, eggs on a shelf.
Thirteen, fourteen, fruit we're sorting.
Fifteen, sixteen, cake is mixing.
Seventeen, eighteen, dinner's waiting.
Nineteen, twenty, we have plenty.

Skip Counting Rhymes

Rhymes are used again in this fun method to teach children skip counting. When body movements or clapping patterns are added, all learning styles will respond!

Counting by Two: This rhyme is fun to act out while saying it aloud. On the "hip hop" the children hop twice, then act out whatever the line says. This is a great activity for kinesthetic learners.

Hip hop **two**, buckle my shoe.

Hip hop **four**, close the door.

Hip hop **six**, pick up sticks.

Hip hop **eight**, lay them straight.

Hip hop **ten**, a big, fat hen.

Hip hop **twelve**, eggs on a shelf.

Hip hop **fourteen**, fruit we're sorting.

Hip hop **sixteen**, cake is mixing.

Hip hop **eighteen**, dinner's waiting.

Hip hop **twenty**, we have plenty.

Counting by Three: Pick 12 children to stand in front of the class and each child holds a large 9" x 12" piece of colored paper with one of the numbers of this rhyme written on it in black marker. As the class says their number the child quickly holds it up high and then brings it back down. Everyone participates saying the rhyme aloud.

Three, six, nine,
I feel so fine.

Twelve, fifteen, eighteen,
I'm making a painting.

Twenty-one, twenty-four, twenty-seven,
I paint a picture that looks like heaven.

Thirty, thirty-three, thirty-six,
I frame my picture with 4 little sticks!

Counting by Four: This rhyme is fun to say aloud while clapping it out to the beat.

Four, eight, whoops I'm late.
Twelve, sixteen, watch needs fixing.
Twenty, twenty-four, here I come, through the door.
Twenty-eight, thirty-two, teacher says "shame on you".
Thirty-six, forty, friends call me "Shorty".

Counting by Five: Use a "sing-song" voice and clap to the syllables.

Five, ten,	(2) slow claps
Fifteen, twenty,	(4) even claps
Twenty-five, thirty,	(3) fast, (2) even claps
Thirty-five, forty,	(3) fast, (2) even claps
Forty-five, fifty,	(3) fast, (2) even claps
Fifty-five, sixty,	(3) fast, (2) even claps
Sixty-five, seventy,	(3) fast, (2) even claps
Seventy-five, eighty,	(3) fast, (2) even claps
Eighty-five, ninety,	(3) fast, (2) even claps
Ninety-five, one hundred!	(3) fast, (3) even claps

Counting by Ten:
Since counting by ten is easily remembered, it is fun to have the class practice saying it aloud, while exercising.

Ten, twenty,	Touch each foot.
Thirty, forty,	Touch each knee.
Fifty, sixty,	Touch each hip.
Seventy, eighty,	Touch each shoulder.
Ninety, one-hundred.	Touch each ear, and put hands up.

No More Counting on Fingers!

Memorizing Addition and Subtraction Facts

Teaching children to memorize addition and subtraction facts is not an easy task! There are approximately 180 different combinations of numbers to remember from any number plus or minus 1 through 18.

Usually adding and subtracting by 1 is easy for children as long as they are proficient in sequencing forward and backward. We give children many different methods to use to figure out the answer, but most of these methods such as "Touch Math" and using a number line or even counting on fingers, take too much time. The goal is to have children <u>memorize</u> all the facts and have instant recall. But as teachers or parents we don't know how to teach them to memorize.

The memorization method presented in this section is based on the "fact family" idea. That means teaching adding and subtracting as a group or family.

$$2 + 8 = 10 \qquad 10 - 2 = 8$$
$$8 + 2 = 10 \qquad 10 - 8 = 2$$

Learning that these three numbers are linked together is the beginning of the process. Since rhymes are powerful tools for auditory learners and pictures aid the visual learner, the fact family can be put to rhyme along with a picture and a clapping pattern added for the kinesthetic learner. This is how it works. The rhyme goes like this:

<table>
<tr><td>

2 + 8 is 10
I'm in a lion's den
10 - 8 is 2
He started to nibble
my shoe!

</td><td>

</td></tr>
</table>

Show the picture to the students and have them say the rhyme in a "sing-song" manner while clapping out the rhythm at the same time. It's fun to do and the children will want to do it again and again! Every time they say it aloud it is being etched into long-term memory. Now have them find a partner and make up their own clapping patterns. Try using the rhymes for a jump rope game.

The key to this method of association of the fact family numbers, is through repetition. Do not introduce a new rhyme until the current one is well established and that information is being transferred to practical usage.

The concept behind all this fun, is that the students are making an association between the three numbers in the fact family. They are remembering that 2, 8 and 10 belong together as a family. Now, there is a connection! Educators are convinced that the fact family method is highly successful in learning.

This technique is beneficial for all the learning styles, especially the verbal/auditory learner and kinesthetic learner. The picture helps the visual learner, but it is also suggested that they draw and color the picture themselves and write the rhyme.

Rhymes can be made up for each fact family, along with a simple drawing. But if you aren't so inclined, there is a reasonable product available called Memory Joggers Addition and Subtraction Learning System that uses this method. It comes with a 66 page Activity Book to reinforce and assess the child's progress, plus a CD and complete Parent/Teacher Guide. (See Product Resources.)

Addition Words
Children have a difficult time remembering the meanings of words that pertain to the skill of adding and subtracting. Word problems can be confusing if children don't understand the meaning of the word and are not able to identify the procedure to use for solving the problem.

Putting the terms in rhyme,
helps the child define!

Unfamiliar math vocabulary words in word problems often confuse students. The following are some of the more common "hard to remember" words found in addition and subtraction word problems.

There were 15 green apples in a basket and 13 red apples. Find the <u>sum</u> of all the apples. If the child has memorized the simple little rhyme below, it clarifies the process immediately. (Point out to the child that "sum" should be spelled "some" in the context of the rhyme.)

"<u>Sum</u>" apples are green,
"<u>Sum</u>" apples are red.
<u>Sum</u> is the answer,
When you add in your head.

Another term that appears to be confusing to some children is "in all". If they know this simple two line rhyme, the procedure in this word problem makes sense. Mary had 3 balls and Jimmy had 4. How many balls were there <u>in all</u>?

How many balls <u>in all</u>?
We add to get the call.

Bob's dog had 6 bones. Mario's dog had 3 bones. What was the <u>total</u> number of bones?

<u>Total</u> is an adding word
That is what I overheard.

Jenny and Mark were making snow balls. Jenny made 12 snow balls. Mark made 9. How many snow balls did they make <u>altogether</u>?

How many snow balls <u>altogether</u>?
Add them up in snowy weather.

Subtraction Words

Joe's dog weighs 12 pounds. Carol's dog weighs 4 pounds. What is the <u>difference</u> in their weights?

<u>Difference, difference</u>, what can it be?
The subtraction answer, don't you see?

Calvin carried 20 glasses to the table. 8 fell and broke. How many were <u>left</u>?

Mr. Potter drove 423 miles on his vacation. Mrs. Jones drove 398 miles on her vacation. How many miles <u>less</u> did Mrs. Jones drive?

<u>Left</u> and <u>Less</u> mean take-away
Get it right every day!

Jill ran a race in 9 minutes. Kara ran it in 13 minutes. <u>How many more</u> minutes did it take Kara to run the race?

<u>How many more</u> can it be?
Use subtraction and you'll see.

Subtraction Cues

A quick way to help children remember whether it is necessary to regroup (borrow) in a subtraction problem, is by having them say this mnemonic phrase to themselves.

"Bigger Bottom, Better Borrow"
43
-27

By calling the student's attention to the number on the bottom (the 7), and determining if it is bigger than the top number (the 3), the children will be able to easily decide whether or not to borrow or regroup.

> *Memory Tip:*
> *Registration in long-term memory is enhanced*
> *when problems are solved forwards and backwards.*
> *Work the problem to find the answer,*
> *and then take your answer*
> *and work back to the original problem.*

Place Value

Color Coding Columns

It's a good idea to color code the ones', tens' and hundreds' column if your student has difficulty keeping numbers lined up. It works well to use large graphing paper for writing the problem.

Color the ones' column numbers using green because green means "go" or "start". Use different colors for the tens and hundreds column. Draw a green arrow to indicate where to start in the ones column.

Word Problems

Visual learners and dyslexic children frequently need pictures to help them visualize the word problem and understand the solution. Encourage students to make simple drawings of word problems. Teachers who employ this method help engage <u>all</u> the students with understanding. Pictures also help to capture the attention of children who are restless and need a focal point.

By teaching students to draw pictures of the problems on their own, they will learn how to analyze the problem and solve it. It makes more sense if they can see it. There are some good books available for different grade levels, called *Read It! Draw It! Solve It!* by Elizabeth Miller. The books contain black line masters for every day of the school year. Students analyze the problem, solve it by drawing and then write their responses. (See Product Resources for more information.)

It is easy to teach children to think of word problems visually. Here are some examples of how to use pictures for word problems.

Karen has 6 boxes of cookies. There are 4 cookies in each box. How many cookies does Karen have?

Many children will consider adding 6 + 4. But by visualizing and drawing the problem they can quickly see the necessity for multiplication.

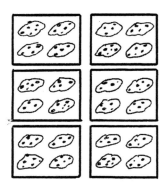

There will always be some problems that are not easily drawn because of large numbers. In these cases it is still necessary to encourage the students to begin the drawings until they realize the mathematical process to use.

This example shows the beginning of the drawing process.

Maria put 8 sketches on each page of her sketch book. She drew 56 sketches. How many pages did she fill?

$$56 \div 8 = 7$$

If the visual learner doesn't "see" the first page, he/she may try to solve the problem by adding 56 + 8, or multiplying 56 x 8. Once a visual is provided, the procedure becomes more apparent to the student.

Sean has 13 marbles in one jar and 5 marbles in another jar. He wants the same number of marbles in each jar. What is the fewest number of marbles that must be moved?

This problem may best be solved by doing a hands-on demonstration, followed by groups working together to solve the problem. Fill one clear jar with 13 marbles and another with 5. Have the kinesthetic learners demonstrate how to solve the problem by moving the marbles. Visual learners may need to actually draw pictures of the procedure. Explain the different mathematical methods for obtaining the solution.

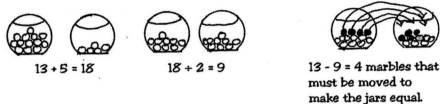

13 + 5 = 18   18 ÷ 2 = 9   13 - 9 = 4 marbles that must be moved to make the jars equal.

Visual and tactile learners may want to use this method:

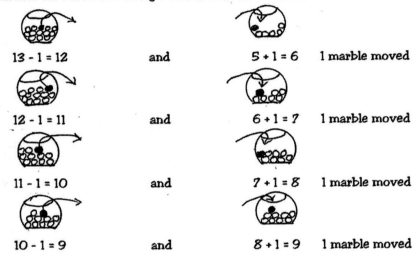

13 - 1 = 12	and	5 + 1 = 6 1 marble moved
12 - 1 = 11	and	6 + 1 = 7 1 marble moved
11 - 1 = 10	and	7 + 1 = 8 1 marble moved
10 - 1 = 9	and	8 + 1 = 9 1 marble moved

Thus, 4 marbles were moved.
This problem is another example where a sketch clarifies the procedure.

Five out of seven students in a class like to solve math puzzles. There are 28 students in the class. How many of them like to solve math puzzles?

O O O O O O O   O O O O O O O
1 2 3 4 5   1 2 3 4 5

O O O O O O O   O O O O O O O
1 2 3 4 5   1 2 3 4 5

5 x 4 = 20

A train starts at Damascus and makes stops at Evanston and Frederick on its journey to Gaithersburg. The route is 25 miles long. If it is 6.2 miles from Damascus to Evanston and 8.3 miles from Frederick to Gaithersburg, how far is it from Evanston to Frederick?

D   E   F   G

I 6.2   I   I 8.3   I

6.2	25.0	It is 10.5 miles from
+8.3	- 14.5	Evanston to Frederick
14.5	10.5	

Many visual learners do poorly in math unless they can actually "see" the problem. It is difficult for visual learners to conceptualize problems accurately. Once they understand by "seeing" it is easy to find the correct method for solving the problem.

The visual learner needs to be taught how to put a word problem into a drawing. Teachers often feel they aren't good at drawing and hesitate showing a student visually how to work the problem. But as can be seen from the previous sketches, the pictures only need to be representations. The simpler the drawing, the faster the student can solve the problem. Don't leave these visual learners behind and lost!

It is the supreme art of the teacher
to awaken joy in creative
expression and knowledge.
Albert Einstein

My, How Time Flies!

Days of the Week

Remembering the days of the week in order are sometimes a challenge. Rhymes are very helpful in this type of sequencing. Children will learn this rhyme quickly and easily.

Days of the Week Rhyme

Sunday learn the Golden Rule.
Monday off we go to school.
Tuesday is a day to add.
Wednesday we are kind of bad.
Thursday teacher gives a test.
Friday we will do our best.
Saturday is here for play.
Now you know the seven days.

Reproduce pages found in **Appendix C** (pages 124 – 132.) to make a "Days of the Week Rhyme Book." Assemble by stapling together and add a colorful cover. Instruct children to copy the rhyme on the appropriate lines and color the picture. Repeat the rhyme aloud numerous times and clap out the syllables. This is an excellent activity to do when you are studying calendars.

Making a calendar for each month is a nice activity too. It helps children learn the idea of planning and looking ahead. The calendar can be filled in with birthdays during the month, holidays, due dates of projects etc.

By taping a calendar on each student's desk, it becomes a handy reference, or staple 12 pages together in book form. Students can design the heading area, write the name of each month and fill in the dates. Use the calendar master to reproduce. (See **Appendix D** on page 133.)

Memory Tip:
Rhymes are powerful!
Remembering one rhyming word
Jogs your memory into recalling others.

Calendar Months

This familiar rhyme helps children learn how many days are in each month. This is another example of the powerful influence of rhymes. Most adults know and use this old English rhyme all their lives.

How Many Days?

30 days hath September,
April, June and November.
All the rest have 31.
(Except February which has 28
and sometimes 29.)

Knuckle Method for Days in a Month

Another method for remembering the days of the month is the "Knuckle Method". Count the months across your knuckles (at the base of your fingers), both on the top of the knuckles and between the knuckles.

Starting on the left, the first knuckle corresponds to January (and has 31 days), the indentation between the first and second knuckles is February (with 28 days), the second knuckle is March (with 31), then the indentation is April (30), the third knuckle is May (31), the next indentation is June (30), and the fourth knuckle is July (31).

Now go to the right hand, and start out with a knuckle for August (31), then September (30), then October (31), then November (30), then December (31). It is easy to remember that knuckles are the months with 31 days and the indentations between are 30 days (except February).

If students are curious why our calendar is so confusing, encourage them to search under Roman calendar history on the Internet.

A Rhyme to Teach the Months in Order

Rhymes are helpful in teaching all of the months in order. By repeating this rhyme frequently, the sequencing will come naturally.

Have students make up rhyme books, writing the rhymes and illustrating the pages. Combining math with language arts integrates the teaching.

Use rhymes as a choral reading activity, dividing the class into groups to read a paragraph in unison. The more times something is repeated aloud the better chance of it being retained in long term memory. It also aids the audio learners to hear the rhyme repeated many times.

Months in Order

January, February,
March and April too,
The first four months
Bring happiness to you,

May and June,
July and August
Lots of fun when
the summer's hottest,

September, October,
The leaves are falling,
November, December,
Holidays are calling.

These 12 months
are easy to remember
52 weeks from
Jan. to December.

How many days
in a year?
three hundred sixty five
Is that clear?

Let's Make a Clock!

Visual and tactile learners need a hands-on experience with clocks. Use the clock face (**Appendix E** on page 134) and assemble it by following the directions.

Use the clock by setting the hands for these activities:

Set the clocks for a particular time.

Use the clock to observe the passage of time.

Move the hands backward to discover an earlier time.

At the beginning of the day, post the starting times for classroom activities on the board. Ask how long it will be until recess or lunch etc. By keeping the clock handy on the desktop, students will be encouraged to use it to solve time problems. The verbal/auditory learners will want to talk to others or themselves in order to understand the clock. Audio learners are good at teaching others and this helps to solidify their understanding too.

Another relevant activity for learning the passage of time is by providing a copy of a TV schedule. Ask questions about the programs on the schedule.

What time will _____ end?

How long in hours and minutes is the movie on Channel 7 at 8:00?

If you have to go to bed at 9:00 P.M., will you be able to see all of _____ ?

Encourage students to use either the clocks to solve the problems, or draw pictures for understanding, or verbally count the hours and minutes. By recognizing and encouraging all different modes of learning, each student will benefit.

Hour and Minute Hands

Children frequently confuse the minute hand and hour hand. A good way to distinguish the difference is by pointing out that the hour hand is shorter because it points to the numbers which are closer to the center of the clock than the minutes. The minute hand is longer because it has to reach out and almost touch the minute designations.

Another method is to color the minute designations red and the minute hand red. Visual learners like to use color to make distinctions. As they become comfortable telling time, they will no longer need the colors.

Become a Clock!
This is a fun method for learning to tell time that engages all the kinesthetic learners. Clear a floor area or do this activity outside. Pick 12 students to hold hands while stretched out in a large circle. Students face towards the center and drop hands.

Teacher gives each student a sheet of paper with a number (from 1 to 12). Each student repeats his number as the teacher walks around the inside of the circle in a clockwise direction, just as the hands of a clock move.

One student is picked to stand in the very center of the circle with one arm outstretched, representing the hour hand. He has a large paper sign with H for hour attached to his chest. Another student stands with her arm outstretched closer to the outer part of the circle representing the minute hand and wears an M for minute.

The teacher calls out a time such as 4:35. The "hour student" points to a little past the four and the "minute student" begins at the 12 and counts aloud by fives walking around the circle and points to the correct minute time. Students decide if the time is correct. Alternate so all children have an opportunity to be a minute or hour hand.

The more connections that can be made in the brain,
the more integrated the experience is within memory.
Don Campbell

Time Changes

To remember how to adjust clocks for Daylight and Standard Time, use this slogan:

Spring ahead,

Fall back

A.M./P.M.

12:01 midnight to 12:00 noon are A.M. hours

12:01 noon to 12:00 midnight are P.M. hours.

A.M./P.M. designations are more easily remembered if a picture is drawn showing what occurs during that time. Divide a 12" x 18" sheet of drawing paper into 1-1/2" increments the long way. Fold so that there are 12 sections. Fold the paper again the "hot dog" way. Now you have 24 sections. Label the sections as indicated. The children draw pictures of what might occur during those hours in their life. Color all the AM pictures in one color and the PM pictures in a different color.

Is It Odd or Even?

Odd and Even Activities

Counting by two is an easy method to distinguish odd or even numbers.
2, 4, 6, 8, 10 are all even numbers. Any number ending in any of these numbers are even. Odd numbers are all the rest!

24 - EVEN because it ends with 4
180 - EVEN because it ends with 0
265 - ODD because it ends with 5
10,244,683 - ODD because it ends with 3

Remember, rhymes are beneficial for audio learners. Add clapping to the rhyme and kinesthetic learners are involved.

> 2, 4, 6, 8, 10 - even numbers, say it again!
> 1, 3, 5, 7, 9 - odd numbers, out of line!

This is another activity that is good for kinesthetic learners. It works best outside. All students stand in a line. By linking arms with as many others as they want, they decide if they are odd or even. One side can be the Even Area and another the Odd Area. They continue changing partners and running to the correct area. Children love the activity and quickly understand the odd/even concept.

Another method is to have the child say "one" with a closed fist turned to show the fingers. Then the fist is turned over at "two" so the back of the hand shows. The hand continues turning over, back and forth as the numbers are spoken. When the back of the hand is on top, it's an even number.

Literature tie in: Read *The Crayon Counting Book* by Pam Munoz Ryan. It's about counting odd and even numbers and is a good follow up. Another cute story book is *Odd Todd and Even Steven* by Kathryn Cristaldi.

Picture This for Rounding Numbers

The easiest way to teach rounding is by using a picture.

Draw a mountain on the board or on a long piece of paper. Put 0, 10, 20, 30 in the valley depressions and 5, 15 and 25 at the top of each peak. Write the numbers 1 - 4 up the left side of the mountain and 6 – 9 etc. on the right side of the mountain.

If you have a white board and can use magnets, cut a small car out of a magazine and mount the magnet on the back. Pick a number between 1-9.

Begin the trip with the car going up the mountain. If the number ends in 1 - 4, drive the car to that number, get out to look at the view and forget to put on the brake. Ask the students what happens to the car if it's brake is not on, and the students will respond that the car will roll. Discuss whether it will roll up the hill to the next number or back down to the lower number. Talk about the fact that a car won't roll up so the number rounds to the lower number.

If the number ends in 6 - 9, repeat the process with the car. Discuss whether it will roll forward or backward, and round to the higher number. If the number is 5, we determine that the engine end of the car probably weighs more than the empty trunk, so the car will roll forward to the higher number. Adjust the numbers as you progress in rounding to tens, hundreds, and thousands.

Non-Visual Method

Some learners respond to procedural methods. Try this one if your student prefers a more rule-based technique.

What is 27 rounded to the nearest 10?

Underline the digit in the tens place,	2 7
Circle the digit to the right of it,	2 ⑦
Is the circled digit five or more?	Yes
Then change the underlined digit to the next higher number and add a zero,	3 0

What is 52 rounded to the nearest 10?

Underline the digit in the tens place.	5 2
Circle the digit to the right of it,	5 ②
Is the circled digit five or more?	No
Then leave the underlined digit and change the circled digit to zero.	5 0

The circled digit will always be changed to zero, thus the circle represents a zero. The only decision making required is with the underlined number. If it's 5 or more, the circled digit increases. If it is under 5, it stays the same.

What is 684 rounded to the nearest hundred?

Underline the digit in the hundreds place.	6 8 4
Circle the digit to the right of it.	6 ⑧ 4
Is the circled digit 5 or more?	Yes
Then change the underlined digit to the next higher digit and change the other digits to zero.	7 0 0

What is 943? rounded to the nearest hundred?

Underline the digit in the hundreds place.	9 4 3
Circle the digit to the right of it.	9 ④ 3
Is the circled digit 5 or more?	No
Then leave the underlined digit and change the other digits to zero.	9 0 0

Rounding Game (works well with children who learn kinesthetically)

1. Pick 2 children to hold large cards with the numbers 10, and 20 written on each one.

2. Pick 9 other children and give them cards with the remaining numbers, 11, 12, 13, 14, 15, 16, 17, 18, and 19.

3. Call the numbers randomly. Each child comes up to take their proper place, behind the 10 or behind the 20, depending on the rounding of their number to the nearest 10. Make sure each student says his/her number and the reason for choosing the 10 or 20 to stand behind.

4. If children are confused, call on audio learners to help. The verbal students need to talk in order to process the information.

This game is an excellent way to introduce rounding.

Memory Tip:
Remember, it is easier for the brain
to retain information if the term is said aloud.
Often we think "silence is golden" in the classroom,
but it is necessary for students to speak
and hear themselves say the information aloud.

3M's and an R (Mean, Median, Mode, Range)

Here is a set of numbers: 58, 70, 70, 108, 84, 90. They might be math grades, for example. The **MEAN** is the same as average. Most students are familiar with the term "average" so the memory tip for connecting the word MEAN to AVERAGE is easy. Draw an average guy - not too tall, not too thin, just average. Now draw a mean look on his face. When the student is asked to find the MEAN of a list of numbers, the picture of the mean, <u>average</u> guy will pop into his head and he will remember that MEAN is the same as average.

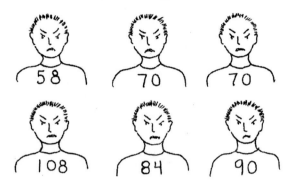

To average or find the MEAN, add together all of the numbers and then divide it by the sum of the total number.
Using this set of data: 58, 70, 70, 108, 84, 90.
 By adding the numbers, the answer is 480. Divide by 6 (numbers) = 80

The **MEDIAN** is the 'middle value' in your list. The word sounds similar to the word "middle." That makes it easy to remember the process.

Step 1: Put the numbers in order from lowest to highest.
58,   70,   70,   84,   90,   108

Step 2: Count how many numbers there are. <u>6</u>

Step 3: Since 6 is an even number, the median is equal to the sum of the two middle numbers divided by two. 70 + 84 = 154 ÷ 2 = <u>77</u>

When the total digits of the list are odd, as in this list: (7 numbers)
58,   70,   70,   84,   90,   108,   110
The median is the middle entry in the list after sorting the list into increasing order. The median is 84.   Be sure to remember the odd and even rule.

The **MODE** is the value that occurs most often.

58, 70, 70, 108, 84, 90

In this case, since there are (2) 70's, the mode is 70.   To remember the word MODE, think about the first two letters in the word MODE, MO. If you add ST you would have MOST which is the meaning of MODE (the value that occurs MOST often!)

<u>M O</u> D E   <u>M O</u> S T

It is important to note that there can be more than one mode and if no number occurs more than once in the set, then there is no mode for that set of numbers.

The **RANGE** is the difference between the lowest and highest values.

Using this data: 56, 70, 70, 100, 84, 80

The highest value is 100 and the lowest is 56. 100 - 56 = 44, so the range is 44. The range tells you something about how spread out the data are. Data with large ranges tend to be more spread out.

The word RANGE brings to mind cowboys out on the range, open and spread out. Have the students draw a picture of cowboys out on the range, each with a different number on their hat. Circle the highest number and lowest number. Subtract.

100 - 56 = 44

Money Makes the World Go Around!

Coin Rhyme
Try teaching this poem to reinforce coin recognition. (From atozkidsstuff.com)
As the children say the poem, they must find the appropriate coin.

Penny, penny,
Easily spent
Copper brown
and worth one cent.

Nickel, nickel,
Thick and fat,
You're worth five cents.
I know that.

Dime, dime,
Little and thin,
I remember,
You're worth ten.

Quarter, quarter
Big and bold,
Worth twenty-five
I am told!

Teaching Money in the Classroom....this makes "cents"!!

Teaching students about money can be a headache! Especially if you are using work sheets where even <u>you</u> aren't sure if the fuzzy picture is a quarter or a nickel. Boring! Kids like money, even play money. Often teachers buy the fake currency and coins and there it sits on a shelf. How do you use it to make it fun and a great learning experience?

The best way to teach currency/coin recognition, money value and making change, is by using play money in the classroom or home in real life circumstances. There are three basic premises to teach about money. How it is **earned**, how it can be **saved** and prudent **spending**.

Objectives of Money System:

1. Students learn how to recognize coin value.
2. Subtraction skills are employed in making change.
3. Students have an opportunity to see the value in saving money for a future goal.
4. Children learn how to fill out job applications.
5. Students are allowed to make decisions on how they spend their money.
6. Accounting skills are learned by doing.
7. Children learn how an auction functions.

Earning Money

Students earn money by good attendance, performing a classroom job, turning in homework on time and by earning interest on their savings.

How the System Works

Give each student a set amount of play cash and coins at the beginning of the year, to be kept in a zip bag in their desk. It is their responsibility to keep it safe, just as it is in real life.

Decide on types of classroom jobs, such as line leader, window opener, messenger etc. Make up a Classified Ad for Help Wanted. (See **Appendix G** on page 136.) It gives ideas of possible job listings and the format to use. Determine the salary for each job. It is easier if you only change jobs every 2 weeks.

To be hired for a job, students must fill out a job application. (See **Appendix F** on page 135.) This teaches students how to fill out forms, to remember their address and how to express themselves in writing.

The key to making this system easy for the teacher, is by picking at least one very responsible Accountant. The two accountants, pay everyone according to the money earned from their jobs and also 5 cents for every day they come to school on time.

Students can earn money by turning in homework on time. The Homework Checker keeps track, and informs the teacher which students earn a bonus of 25 cents.

Saving Money

Discuss the importance of maintaining a savings account. Talk about larger purchases later or keeping money for a "rainy day". The teacher is the banker and keeps track of the money in each student's savings account. Often a parent helper can be in charge of the record keeping for the savings account. Depending on the grade level, teach students how to calculate interest and explain how it compounds.

Spending Money
Money can be spent for drinks of water, a new pencil or box of crayons or anything the teacher deems practical. Students learn coin recognition very quickly this way. If they want to buy a pencil for 25 cents and present a dollar bill, the child must know how much change they will receive or they are sent back to their seat to figure it out. Adjust these ideas to the grade level of the child.

At the end of each month, an auction is held. This is the part children love! Students bring in old toys, books, things they no longer want (with their parents permission!) and an auction is held. First they must count their money and decide how much they are willing to spend. They look over the items on display and decide on which they will bid. The teacher opens bidding for items, staying within 5 cent increments. It is a lot of fun and it's amazing how quickly addition and subtraction skills are improved. At the end of the auction, students count their money and decide if their purchases were wise.

This hands-on approach to teaching money is fun, easy and educational. Students have an ownership of the process and are anxious to learn how to identify the coins, make change and count their money. This method is easy to set up and affords students a daily practice of using money.

Memory Tip:
Tell me and I'll forget.
Show me, and I may not remember.
Involve me, and I'll understand and
remember.

Throw the Times Table Chart Away!

Memorizing Multiplication and Division Facts

The memorization process comes <u>after</u> students are taught the concept of multiplication and division, using manipulatives and other methods of teaching. Begin teaching multiplication by pointing out groups of things. Teach the difference between a group and an array by drawing pictures.

Group - an irregular arrangement of numbers or symbols.

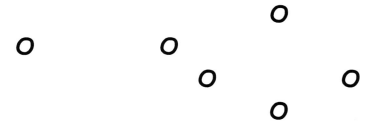

Array - a systematic arrangement of numbers or symbols in rows or columns
"Hooray! Array! We march in a parade!

Continue to explain that multiplication is simply a faster way of adding. Once they understand the concept of multiplication and division, proceed to the memorization methods as outlined here.

> *Memory Tip:*
> *Understanding must be the foundation*
> *and memorization the process.*

After teaching children to memorize addition and subtraction facts, it seems overwhelming to have to teach all of the multiplication and division facts from 0 through 12. Mnemonics, using associations, stories and rhymes are very effective in the memorizing process.

The memorization method presented in this section is based on the "fact family" idea. That means teaching multiplication and division as a group or family and both at the same time. Learning that the three numbers in the fact family are associated, is the beginning of the process.

$$3 \times 4 = 12 \qquad\qquad 12 \div 3 = 4$$
$$4 \times 3 = 12 \qquad\qquad 12 \div 4 = 3$$

Teaching How to Multiply by Zero

How many times do students incorrectly answer $4 \times 0 = 4$??? They have been adding $4 + 0 = 4$ for so long that it seems natural to them that $4 \times 0 = 4$. For some reason our logical teaching does not get through to many students. These students need a method that they can remember and not become confused. By using the association idea, think of the zero as a mouth.

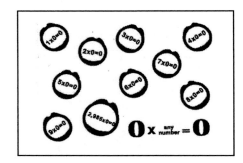

Explain to the students that since a mouth eats things, it will eat every other number and all that remains is the 0 or the mouth. Children will quickly visualize this idea and grasp the concept. Instruct them to draw hungry mouths on their paper and write as many equations they can think of, using all the numbers from 1 - 9 and then any other numbers of their choice.

Draw a large zero with lips on a piece of cardboard and have the tactile learners toss numbers into the mouth while making up a zero fact. Follow up by writing the equation. Any number $\times$ 0 = 0.

Multiplying and Dividing by One

One sounds a little like "gum" and looks like a stick of gum. Beginning with this sound-alike association between 1 and gum, explain that once gum has been chewed it becomes very sticky and sticks to things or to the other number and becomes a part of the other number. In the example $1 \times 4 = 4$, the one (gum) is stuck to the four and all that remains is the four.

$$1 \times 4 = 4$$

In order to visualize this association, draw the 4 as a door (door is the sound-alike for 4) and draw the gum stuck to the door and leaving only the 4.

Follow up by writing the fact family:

1 x 4 = 4	4 ÷ 1 = 4
4 x 1 = 4	1 ÷ 4 = not possible as a whole number.

Explain, using fractions, why 1 cannot be divided by 4 and equal a whole number. Illustrate using a piece of paper as the one. If it were divided by 4, it would become a fraction (not a whole number) and would equal 1/4.

Multiplying and Dividing by Two

Counting by two is an easy method for learning to multiply and divide by two. Usually by the time multiplication is introduced, most students know how to count by two.

In some cases, children understand more easily if they think of 2 x 6 as six added two times (6 + 6). Whichever method is used, it is important to teach the fact family along with it, so division can be taught at the same time. If a review is needed for counting by two, use a counting rhyme.

Counting by Two: Use this Counting by Two. It is fun to act out the rhyme while saying it aloud. On the "hip hop" the children hop twice, then act out whatever the line says. This is a good activity for kinesthetic learners.

Hip hop **two**, buckle my shoe,

Hip hop **four**, close the door.

Hip hop **six**, pick up sticks.

Hip hop **eight**, lay them straight.

Hip hop **ten**, a big, fat hen.

Hip hop **twelve**, eggs on a shelf.

Hip hop **fourteen**, fruit we're sorting.

Hip hop **sixteen**, cake is mixing.

Hip hop **eighteen**, dinner's waiting.

Hip hop **twenty**, we have plenty.

Dividing by Two

Working a division problem such as 14 ÷ 2 = ___?___, instruct the student to turn the problem around ___?___ x 2 = 14? What times 2 equals 14? This seems to be an easier method for understanding.

Multiplying and Dividing by Five

Multiplying and dividing by five is an easy task when it is associated with a clock. Since children are comfortable counting by five around the clock, it is the perfect tool to use. The Multiplication Clock below, illustrates how it works.   Using a clock is helpful because it not only teaches multiplication and division but reinforces telling time.   See **Appendix E** for a clock pattern. This is a useful tool for teaching the five's.

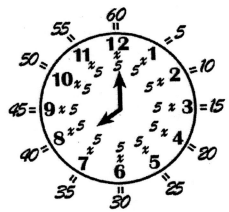

The counter part for division can be easily remembered by noticing the dividend that ends with a zero or five will be a clock problem.

$$3\underline{5} \div 7 = 5$$
$$4\underline{0} \div 5 = 8$$

Using the fact family teaching method makes the process easier and much quicker.

9 x 5 = 45	45 ÷ 5 = 9
5 x 9 = 45	45 ÷ 9 = 5

Counting by Five - Review counting by 5 with this active rhyme. It's fun to do it as a P.E. activity. Use a "sing-song" voice and clap to the syllables.

Five, ten,	(2) slow claps
Fifteen, twenty,	(4) even claps
Twenty-five, thirty,	(3) fast, (2) even claps
Thirty-five, forty,	(3) fast, (2) even claps
Forty-five, fifty,	(3) fast, (2) even claps
Fifty-five, sixty,	(3) fast, (2) even claps
Sixty-five, seventy,	(3) fast, (2) even claps
Seventy-five, eighty,	(3) fast, (2) even claps
Eighty-five, ninety,	(3) fast, (2) even claps
Ninety-five, one hundred!	(3) fast, (3) even claps

Multiplying and Dividing by 3, 4, 6, 7, 8, 9

In the past, multiplying and dividing by **3, 4, 6, 7, 8 and 9** have been the difficult facts to memorize. Not so anymore, using what is called the **Peg System**. In this system, items that are to be memorized are hooked by vivid mental images onto the "pegs" that have already been learned. These are the peg words for learning how to multiply or divide by 3, 4, 6, 7, 8 or 9.

Three is a tree
Four is a door
Six is sticks
Seven is a boy named Kevin
Eight is a snowman named Nate
Nine is a porcupine named Nina

All the peg words are concrete nouns that can easily be adapted to a story, rhyme and picture. This association technique works by developing a story based on the three numbers of the fact family. This method has been successfully used in schools and homes to teach multiplication and division.

Sample Story for 7 x 9 = 63

Here is a sample story for the multiplication fact family of 7 x 9 = 63. Remember the peg word for 7 is a boy named Kevin. The peg word for 9 is a porcupine named Nina (Nine-uh). The other part of the association is a "sound-alike" for the product 63 which will be "sticky tree". Using this type of association method is ideal because the division reciprocal is being taught at the same time with the fact family.

$$7 \times 9 = 63 \qquad 63 \div 7 = 9$$
$$9 \times 7 = 63 \qquad 63 \div 9 = 7$$

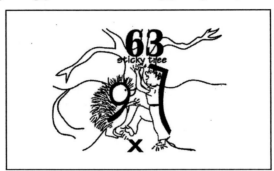

One day Kevin and Nina went for a walk, looking for a tree to climb. They finally found the perfect tree and started to climb it but they got stuck. The tree was covered with sap. It was a "sticky tree" which rhymes with the product, "63".

The reciprocal in the fact family of 63 ÷ 9 = 7 is also easy to recall. "63" reminds the student of "sticky tree" and "9" is Nina, therefore "7" or Kevin is the other character in the story. In about 5 minutes both the multiplication and division facts have been taught without it being a chore!

Stories and rhymes can be made up for each fact family, using the peg system, along with a drawing. But if you aren't so inclined, or don't have the time, there is a product available called Memory Joggers Multiplication and Division Learning System that uses this method. (See Product Resources.)

In order to reinforce the story and have the visual and verbal children take ownership, it is recommended that they use the Memory Joggers Activity book to color the picture and retell the story by writing it. The audio learners should retell the story to others.

Another effective follow-up activity is acting out the stories. Pick 3 children to take the parts of Nina, Kevin and one child to be 63. Pin corresponding numbers on each child. The teacher begins the narration but allows the students to tell the story and act it out verbally. The kinesthetic children love this activity and it is very beneficial to them.

Multiplying by Ten
Tens are easy to teach. Just add a zero to the number being multiplied. Explain it to the students this way:

   10 x 1 = Take the 1 and add a zero = 10
   10 x 20 = Take the 20 and add a zero = 200
   10 x 300 = Take the 300 and add a zero = 3,000

Multiplying by Eleven
Multiplying by eleven for all numbers 1-9, is simple. Double the digit being multiplied.

   11 x 1 = Take the 1 and place another 1 after it = 11
   11 x 2 = Take the 2 and place another 2 after it = 22
   11 x 3 = Take the 3 and place another 3 after it = 33
   etc., etc. up through 9.

Multiplying by 11 (with two digit numbers)
Write the problem: 11 x 10 =
Now write the two outer digits leaving a space between the numbers. 1 ___ 0
Add the two digits: add 1 + 0 = 1
Write the answer of 1 in the space between the two digits: 1 1 0.
The answer to the problem 11 x 10 is 110.

Try this problem: 11 x 11.
Write the outer digits, 1 ___ 1.
Now add the numbers, 1 + 1 = 2
Put the 2 in the space.
The answer to 11 x 11 = 1 2 1

11 x 12
Write 1 ___ 2
Add the numbers, 1 + 2 = 3
Put the 3 in the space. 1 <u>3</u> 2
11 x 12 = 132

Remember, this only works when 11 is written <u>first.</u> (11 x the other number).

Note: This process works up to 11 x 18. After that, use the normal method for multiplying double digits.

$$
\begin{array}{r}
11 \\
\times\ 19 \\
\hline
99 \\
+\ 110 \\
\hline
209
\end{array}
$$

Multiplying by Twelve

By using the peg word "elf" for "12", plus the other known peg words, the facts are recalled by association. "Sound-alikes" are used for the product, to form an association. Stories and rhymes can be made up for each fact family, along with a drawing. But if you aren't so inclined, or don't have the time, this product is included in the *Memory Joggers Multiplying & Dividing Learning System.* (See Product Resources.)

Here's an example of the story for 12 x 2 = 24.

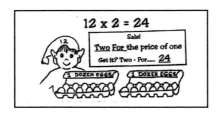

12 sounds like Telf the Elf
2 reminds us of 2 dozen
24 reminds us of the sale "Two for" or 2, 4

Telf, (12) the Elf, loved to grocery shop. He was a real bargain-hunter! One day he noticed that the super market was having a tremendous sale on eggs. Now eggs were one of Telf's favorite foods. He ate them scrambled, fried, poached, soft boiled and hard boiled. He just loved eggs! So when he read in the newspaper that there was a sale:

    2   4

"two for the price of one", he rushed out and bought two (2) dozen eggs.

$$12 \times 2 = 24 \qquad\qquad 24 \div 12 = 2$$
$$2 \times 12 = 24 \qquad\qquad 24 \div 2 = 12$$

Multiplication/Division Terms to Remember

Divisor - The number by which another number is to be divided.
For example: $28 \div 7$ (7 is the divisor or the smaller number)
To remember the difference between the two words, notice that "divis**or**" ends with a small word "**or**." The smaller number is the **divisor**.

Dividend - The number to be divided. For example: $35 \div 5$ (35 is the dividend or the larger number). "Divid**end**" ends with the longer word "**end**." The longer (larger) number is the **dividend**.

Quotient - Quotient (pronounced Kwo-shunt) is the answer after dividing numbers. Again, a silly little rhyme is often helpful to remember the meaning and pronunciation. Students are learning two new vocabulary words; 'quotient', meaning an answer to a division problem and 'absurd' which means silly.

> **Quotient, "kwo-shunt"**
> **What a funny word,**
> **The answer to division**
> **Isn't that absurd?**

To reinforce the division vocabulary and help the visual students see how the words apply to a division problem, place the words in the correct places as shown below.

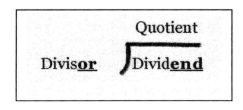

Factors and Product - Factors are numbers that are multiplied together to form a new number called the product. For example: 4 x 3 = 12. The factors are 4 and 3. To help the auditory/verbal student remember this term, say this rhyme:

> **Factors are numbers to multiply**
> **The product's the answer,**
> **Now you know why!**

For the visual learner, label the multiplication sentence. Remember, approximately 60% of the class will be visual learners and they respond to diagrams or seeing a picture.

$$4 \quad x \quad 3 \quad = \quad 12$$

$$\text{factor} \quad x \quad \text{factor} \quad = \quad \text{product}$$
$$\text{or}$$
$$f \quad x \quad f \quad = \quad p$$

Remainder - The number that is left over after dividing. Show this concept visually using manipulatives. Have the children place 7 markers on the desk. Tell them to divide them into 2 equal piles. The one marker <u>remaining</u> is called the <u>remainder.</u> Calling attention to root words help make the terms more meaningful.

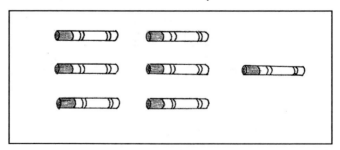

Long Division - To help students remember the sequence of steps in working a long division problem, use this acronym type of association. Introduce "**Dad, Mother, Sister, Brother and their pet dog, Rover.**" The first letter in each word represents a step needed to solve long division problems.

Step 1 - Divide (the D in divide stands for Dad)
Step 2 - Multiply (the M in multiply stands for Mother)
Step 3 - Subtract (the S in subtract stands for Sister)

Step 4 - Bring-down (the B in bring-down stands for Brother)
Step 5 - Remainder (the R in remainder stands for Rover)

Encourage the child to draw the family members in order and write the steps below each picture.

Dad,	Mother,	Sister,	Brother,	Rover
Divide,	Multiply,	Subtract,	Bring-down	Remainder

To make long division easier to teach, use 1/2" square graph paper. By writing the problem with one digit in each square, it is easier for the student to follow the columns when bringing down the next number.

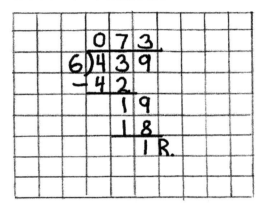

Multiplying positive and negative numbers

This association based on fundamental moral principles helps one to remember the rules for multiplying signed numbers. "Good" things in this association represent positive numbers and "bad" things represent negative numbers.

 X =

A good thing happening to a good person is good.
(Positive times positive equals a positive.)

 X =

A good thing happening to a bad person is bad.
(Positive times negative equals a negative.)

A bad thing happening to a good person is bad.
(Negative times positive equals a negative.)

A bad thing happening to a bad person is good.
(Negative times negative equals a positive.)

Drawing a picture and labeling it with positive or negative signs is helpful. Draw the "bad person" in black and the "good person" in another color. This formula works for division as well.

This little rhyme is helpful too.
Minus times minus is plus,
The reason for this,
we need not discuss.

Mnemonics Number Sense

Digit, Integer, Number and Numeral

What is the difference between a digit, number, numeral and an integer? Not much!! Math terminology can be very confusing to younger students. It is wise to explain they all mean basically the same thing to them. On standardized tests seeing the word integer often causes students to freeze. If the teacher uses the words frequently and points out that they all mean "number," the student becomes more comfortable and can proceed to solve the problem.

Digit - Any of the symbols used to write numbers from 0 to 9. It is called a digit because originally it was related to the fingers. The difference between a digit and a number is that the number has value.

Number - A broad term for the symbols we use to represent arithmetic terms such as value and counting.

> Example of a digit: Write the digit five 5

> Example of a number: Add nine plus two. Now the digits have value and represent the meaning of the number. $9 + 2 = 11$

Numeral - A symbol or mark used to represent a number.   III

Integer - An integer is a positive or negative whole number including 0,

---

Memory Tip:
Just remember digits are like fingers and only go to 10.
You already know what numbers and numerals are!
Integers are positive and negative whole numbers (no fractions).

Number Sentence - a math fact written in horizontal form. Explain that word sentences are written horizontally therefore number sentences are written horizontally too. Sometimes number sentences can have a long sequence of numbers to calculate.

$3 \times 4 = 12$ $7 + 5 - 3 \times 6 \div 9 + 45 - 44 = 7$

Expanded form - A number written as the sum of the values of its digits. Example: 200 + 80 + 7 is the expanded form for 287. Explain the meaning of "expanded" which is to make larger or stretch out. (Stretch or expand a rubber band.) The children can visually see how the number is stretched out in expanded form.

Value - The word value can mean many different mathematical operations and is confusing to children. This term is often used on standardized tests, therefore children need to understand what is being asked. Here is an example of a test question:

"Give the value of the digit 4 in the number 451."

The answer, of course, is 400. The best method for teaching value is with place value markers. By using the manipulatives and explaining that value means recognizing which place the digit is in, (ones, tens, hundreds, thousands etc.), the child can then add the appropriate number of zeros to the digit.

Reading Large Numbers with Ease!
An easy way to teach children how to read large numbers is to explain that the comma will say "thousand" or "million"

23,450 twenty three **thousand** (for the comma), four hundred fifty
895, 721 eight hundred ninety five **thousand** (for the comma), seven hundred twenty one.

3, 430, 299 three **million** (for the comma), four hundred thirty **thousand** (for the comma), two hundred ninety nine.

Greater Than/Lesser Than or Equal
Everyone has their favorite method for remembering these symbols.
> **Greater than**
< **Less than**
= **Equal or same value**

One memory technique that works well, is thinking of > as an arrow shooting or pointing to the smaller number. 234 > 97   97 < 234

Prime Numbers

Prime numbers are best explained using a visual explanation.

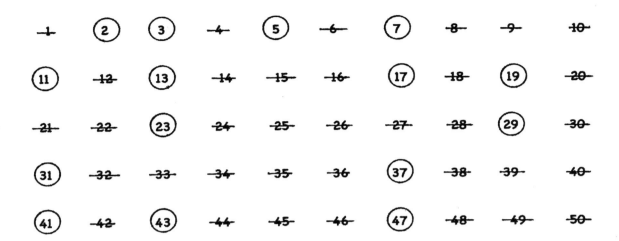

Eratosthenes invented this way to find prime numbers.
From 1 - 50 use this procedure:
Forget 1. Cross it out.
Circle 2. Cross out all numbers divisible by 2.
Circle 3. Cross out all numbers divisible by 3.
Circle 5. Cross out all numbers divisible by 5.
Circle 7. Cross out all numbers divisible by 7.
Since all the remaining numbers are prime, circle them.

All prime numbers are odd except 2 but not all odd numbers are prime numbers. A prime number has **exactly two** factors. The factors are itself and 1.
All the other numbers are **Composite Numbers** and have **more** than 2 factors.

Memory Rhyme to Remember the Prime (Prime Numbers to 50)
2 is the only even prime
3, 5, and 7, 11,
Odd little guys,
13, 17, 19 and 23,
Standing at attention, pleased as can be.
29, 31, and 37, too,
None are divisible, so they're in too,
41, 43, include 47,
This could continue all the way to heaven!

Exponents or Powers

What are exponents and why do we need them? When numbers get really, really big, we need exponents. An exponent tells how many times the base is used as a factor, in other words, how many times the number is multiplied by itself. By writing examples of numbers with exponents, students understand the meaning.

4 to the 4th power
4 = 1st power (we never say 4 to the first power, just leave the number alone)
4 x 4 = 4 to the 2nd power (see the two 4's?)
4 x 4 x 4 = 4 to the 3rd power (notice there are three 4's)
4 x 4 x 4 x 4 = 4 to the 4th power (four 4's being multiplied)

10 to the 7th power
10 x 10 x 10 x 10 x 10 x 10 x 10 = 10,000,000

Square Root

The square root of a number is like having the answer and guessing what the numbers are that produce the answer. What is the square root of 25? What same numbers multiplied together equal 25? 5 x 5 = 25

A square root problem usually looks like this.

$$\sqrt{25}$$

Do not confuse it with the division bracket.

$$5\overline{)25}$$

> *Memory Tip:*
> *Students need to <u>draw</u> the brackets*
> *in order to learn the shapes.*

The following are called **Perfect Squares** and are easily understood when the student draws it on graph paper. By seeing the perfect squares, they realize any number multiplied by itself becomes a **Perfect Square**.

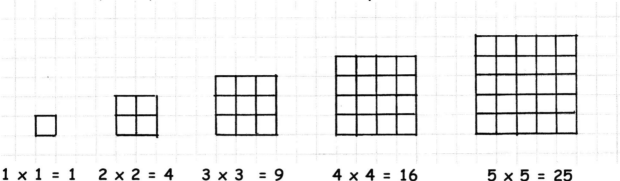

1 x 1 = 1   2 x 2 = 4   3 x 3 = 9   4 x 4 = 16   5 x 5 = 25

Finding the square root of squares that are not perfect is a game of guessing!

Since 12 is not a perfect square, you will use Guess, Divide, Average.
Guess: **3** (3 x 3 = 9) and **4** (4 x 4 = 16)
Divide: 12 ÷ 3 = **4** and 12 ÷ 4 = **3**
Average: 4 + 3 = **7** and next divide by 2 for the two numbers 7 ÷ 2 = **3.5**
Therefore the square root of 12 is approximately 3.5

To make the answer more accurate,
Divide 12 by 3.5 = 3.43
Average 3.5 + 3.43 = 6.93 ÷ 2 = **3.465**

> *Memory Tip:*
> *Remember G, D, A (Guess, Divide, Average)*
> *Continue until you get an accurate number!*

Greatest Common Factors

Greatest Common Factors are the highest numbers that divide exactly into two or more numbers. Remember that it is the "greatest" thing for simplifying fractions! Greatest Common Factor is made up of the words **Factor**, **Common** and **Greatest**.

What is a "Factor"?

A factor is any of the numbers that can be multiplied together to make another number. Factors always occur in pairs. Factors of a number divide the number without a remainder.

> **Memory Tip:**
> The <u>factor</u> (as in Greatest Common Factor)
> is a number that divides into another number exactly.

It is easier to understand by example:
The factors of 12 are 1, 2, 3, 4, 6 and 12 ...

Factors:	Not Factors:
12 ÷ 12 = 1	12 ÷ 11 = 1.09 (not even)
12 ÷ 6 = 2	12 ÷ 10 = 1.2 (not even)
12 ÷ 4 = 3	12 ÷ 9 = 1.33 (not even)
12 ÷ 3 = 4	12 ÷ 8 = 1.5 (not even)
12 ÷ 2 = 6	12 ÷ 7 = 1.71 (not even)
12 ÷ 1 = 12	12 ÷ 5 = 2.4 (not even)

What is a "Common Factor" ?

It is a common factor if it is a factor of two or more numbers - it is then "common to" those numbers.

> **Memory Tip:**
> "Common" means something shared
> or having something in common.

For example, if you work out the factors of two different numbers (say 12 and 30) the common factors are those that are found in both numbers:
The factors of 12 are 1, 2, 3, 4, 6 and 12
The factors of 30 are 1, 2, 3, 5, 6, 10, 15 and 30

Notice that 1, 2, 3 and 6 appear in both lists? So, the common factors of 12 and 30 are: **1, 2, 3**, and **6**.

What is the "Greatest Common Factor" ?

It is simply the largest of the common factors. In our previous example, the largest of the common factors is 6, so the **Greatest Common Factor is 6**.

When the student understands the meaning of the words in the term "Greatest Common Factor or GCF, the process is easier to remember.

Least Common Multiple

The Least Common Multiple (L.C.M.) of two or more numbers is the <u>lowest</u> common multiple that is not zero. It can be used to find the lowest common denominator when adding or subtracting fractions.

Memory Tip:
Least - lowest or smallest.
Common - something shared or in common.
Multiple - what you get when you multiply.

To find the Least Common Multiple of two or more whole numbers, follow this procedure:

1. Make a list of multiples for each whole number.
2. Continue your list until at least two multiples are common to all lists.
3. Identify the common multiples.
4. The Least Common Multiple (LCM) is the smallest of these common multiples.

If we are looking for the common multiples of 12 and 15:

12 x 1 = 12	15 x 1 = 15
12 x 2 = 24	15 x 2 = 30
12 x 3 = 36	15 x 3 = 45
12 x 4 = 48	**15 x 4 = 60**
12 x 5 = 60	

Bingo! The Least Common Multiple of 12 and 15 is 60

Measurement Made Easy

Learning Inch, Foot, Yard and Mile

Stories suggest visual pictures and help children understand terms. In the following story called *King Inch in the Kingdom of Measure* by Donnalyn Yates, children visualize and easily remember the names of customary lengths such as inches, feet, yards and miles. It's fun to read the story aloud while the students illustrate with pictures, labeling the measurement devices. The pictures can later by made into a book. This activity helps children learn to visualize. See the Resource Guide for other math literature book suggestions.

<u>King Inch in the Kingdom of Measure</u>

Long, long ago in the kingdom of Measure, there was a ruler named King Inch. He loved to measure things like the length of his pet dragon or his own big nose or the queen's fingernails. There was only one problem, nothing had been invented to measure with, so he used the tip of his little finger. He would say, "my nose is 3 little finger tips long." He found out his pet dragon was 394 little finger tips long. And on and on he went, measuring everything in sight!

King Inch got tired of saying how many "little finger tips long" everything was. The Queen suggested he name the length after himself. That way people would always think of him. Call the number an "inch."   So from that day on, this length was known as an inch.

One day King Inch wanted to measure his bedroom. He was down on his hands and knees trying to measure with his little finger tip. He gave up and sat down on his bed thinking there must be a better way. Looking at his bare foot gave him an idea! He measured his foot and it was 12 inches long! Now he could walk around and measure things much more easily. He measured his bedroom and it was 16 feet long and 14 feet wide. The king was having such a good time using his feet for measuring.

But sometimes it was hard to measure something tall like a column, with his feet held up in the air. So he had his carpenter make a stick the length of

his foot and his scribes drew 12 inch lines on it. He made a proclamation that 12 inches would always equal 1 foot and since he was the king, it would be called a "ruler." Everyone in his kingdom was excited and began to measure things using their rulers!

One fine day as King Inch was out measuring the castle wall with his little 12 inch ruler, he realized he needed something even longer. He noticed a workman building something with a long stick. Since King Inch was wild about measuring things, he used his little ruler and found out the stick was exactly 3 feet long! He grabbed the stick away from the worker and said,

"This will make my measuring much easier and faster!"

The workman replied, " But good King Inch, I'm building a yard for your dog and I need that stick." The king angrily replied, "Oh, get another yard stick."

And off he went using the yard stick to measure the wall. Soon he began to wonder about something.

"I wonder how many inches are in this yard stick?" said the king aloud. He remembered that the yard stick was exactly 3 feet long. But how many inches would that be? Let's see, 12 inches plus 12 inches plus 12 inches. Or I could multiply 12 x 3.

$$\begin{array}{r} 12 \\ 12 \\ + 12 \\ \hline 36 \end{array} \qquad \begin{array}{r} 12 \\ \times \ \ 3 \\ \hline 36 \end{array}$$

"Ah, a yard stick is 36 inches long or 3 feet long!" exclaimed the king.

King Inch continued to measure. He discovered the wall was 20 yards long. The King wondered how many feet that would equal. He knew his yard stick was 3 feet long so he multiplied 20 yards times 3 feet and it equaled 60 feet.

$$\begin{array}{rl} 20 & \text{yards} \\ \times \ \ 3 & \text{feet} \\ \hline 60 & \text{feet} \end{array}$$

One day, King Inch was invited to Queen Mile's castle. Since he was obsessed with measuring, he ordered a young boy from his kingdom to take the yard stick and start measuring the road from his castle to Queen Mile's castle. As the king rode along comfortably in the horse-drawn coach, the boy was counting how many times he placed the yard stick along the road. He was getting very, very tired but finally they arrived.

The boy stood tall and said "Oh good King Inch, the road to the Queen's castle is 1,760 yards."

The king replied, "No, I want to know how many feet it is to her castle!" Quickly the boy multiplied 1,760 X 3 feet and told the king it was 5,280 feet.

The king was thrilled! He made a proclamation. "From this day forward, 5,280 feet will be called a "mile" since that is how far it is to Queen Mile's castle."

King Inch became known throughout the world. Nothing ever changed. The ruler was always 12 inches long and that measurement was called a foot. The yardstick remained 3 feet long or 36 inches, and the mile equaled 5,280 feet. The Kingdom of Measure will never be forgotten.

King Inch made up this little rhyme to help all of his subjects remember the length of a mile.

Five thousand two hundred and eighty,
The distance to a lovely queen lady,
Her name was Queen Mile
She had a nice smile
Five thousand two hundred and eighty.

Visualizing Liquid Capacity

Cup, pint, quart, half-gallon and gallon are used to measure liquids. Children often have a difficult time remembering these designations. This is an amazing visual to use. Tell this story as the students draw the illustration below.

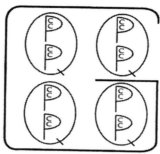

Once in the kingdom of Gallon, (draw a very large G representing the gallon and filling the sheet) **there lived four Queens.** (Draw 4 large Q's to represent the 4 quarts, inside the G.) **Each Queen had a Prince and Princess in her castle.** (Draw 2 P's inside each Q to represent the 2 pints in a quart.) **Each Prince and Princess had 2 cats.** (Draw 2 C's inside each P to represent the 2 cups in a pint.) Point out to the students that the horizontal line on the G shows the division for half gallon.

This visual is highly successful and is easily remembered. The story helps children recall the details as they draw it from memory or see it in their mind.

How Much Does That Weigh?

Ounce, pound and ton are common weights used frequently in daily life. Children need to understand what the weight represents in concrete terms.

Ounce – A file folder weighs approximately one ounce. It is a readily accessible item and 16 folders can be given to each group of children to illustrate the weight of one pound. Write "one ounce" on each folder. Have the groups discover what 8 ounces (1/2 pound) would be or 3 ounces or any designation. Be sure all of the children participate.

one ounce
1 oz.

16 oz. = 1 pound

The abbreviation for ounce is oz. Discuss how strange that abbreviation is. Think of the "land of oz" weighing only one ounce. Draw a tiny magical city perched on a scale and write "oz means ounce." As long as there is some association, terms can be remembered.

Pound – After the children have had an opportunity to "feel" the weight of an ounce, rubber band the folders together and have them make a sign that says "16 ounces = one pound," to be attached to the top of the stack. Make lists of objects that might weigh an ounce and other things that might weigh a pound. Bringing in a scale is very helpful.

As homework, have them look at food packages to discover the weights. Have them feel the weight of one pound of meat at the market or weigh fruit in a hanging scale. What does a bag of 10 pounds of potatoes feel like? Check out the feel of 5 pounds of sugar. This hands-on activity will illustrate the weight of ounces and pounds.

The abbreviation for pound (lb) is even more strange! But there is a reason for it. In England, many years ago, the word for a pound balance on a scale was called "Libra". They took the l and the b from Libra and used them for the abbreviation for pound. Another association might be easier. "lb" could stand for "lovely butter" or "lots of butter". Butter weighs a pound and makes a good association for lb.

Ton - A small car weighs approximately one ton or 2000 pounds. Draw pictures of cars and label them "1 ton or 2000 pounds". Discuss how many file folders it would take to weigh one ton. (About 32,000.) What might weigh 1/2 ton or 1000 pounds? (two motorcycles?)

Investigating Area and Perimeter

Area - The number of square units needed to cover a region.

Graph paper is necessary to teach area. Draw a polygon on the paper, staying on the lines. Instruct the students to count the number of graph squares (or square units) <u>inside</u> the polygon. Discuss the term "square unit". This term is frequently used on standardized tests and will be confusing if the child doesn't understand it's meaning.

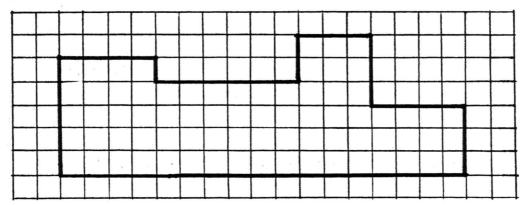

Teach students to multiply the large blocks of area first. Shade this area so the student knows it has been counted.   3 x 17 = 51.

Add the smaller areas: 4 x 2 = 8

                              1 x 6 = 6

                              3 x 3 = 9

                    For a total of 74 sq. units.

Perimeter - The distance around a polygon figure.

The first step to teach with this word, is the correct pronunciation. The word sounds like: per - rim' - uh - ter. Call attention to the small word "rim" found inside pe<u>RIM</u>eter. Talk about the rim of a glass being the outer edge of the glass. Find the word "meter" in peri<u>METER</u>. Discuss the meaning of meter (to measure). So, perimeter means to measure the distance around the edge of something. Find the perimeter of the polygon on the previous page (illustrating area) by adding. Color the outer edge of the polygon with a marker after counting the number of units.

5 + 17 + 3 + 4 + 3 + 3 + 2 + 6 + 1 + 4 = 48 units for the perimeter

Volume

Cubic Unit - is a cube used to measure the volume of a space figure in which cubes fit inside. Sounds confusing but it isn't. It is easily taught using Unifix cubes. The children are familiar with the term "cube" since Unifix cubes have been frequently used. By associating "unit" with "Unifix," children remember the term <u>cubic</u> <u>unit.</u>

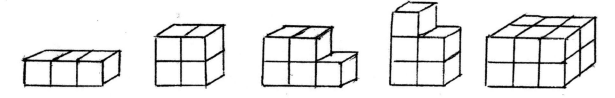

By using Unifix cubes, volume will be more understandable. Have each child form the figures with the Unifix cubes and count the units and say aloud what their findings are. For example, after forming the first figure, they say aloud "the volume is 4 cubic units". Whenever information is repeated aloud numerous times, it is more easily coded in long-term memory.

Unless we remember,
We cannot understand.
Edward Forste

Oh No, Not Metric!

Length

Centimeter – When compared to U.S. Customary Length, a centimeter is a little less than one-half inch. It is about the width of a small finger. This little rhyme may help remember the approximate size of the unit.

My little finger, not wide at all,
A centimeter wide, that is all!!

Meter – When comparing a meter to U.S. Customary Length, a meter is close to a yard. It's actually 39.37 inches. Use this rhyme to help.

A meter measures 3 ft. 3,
It's longer than a yard, you see.

There are 100 centimeters in a meter. Think of a yardstick being 3 inches longer and you will have a meter stick. Take chalk outside and measure one meter lengths. Write "1 meter = 100 centimeters" on each length drawn.

Kilometer - When comparing a kilometer to U.S. Customary Length, a kilometer is very close to a mile. It is 1000 meters. "Kilo" means one thousand. The pronunciation for kilometer should be practiced too. It can be pronounced two different ways and both are correct.
1. kil' - <u>o</u>- me -ter
2. ki - lom' - e - ter

Saying this rhyme will help the student memorize the length.

A kilometer is awfully long
1000 meters
So, don't get it wrong!

Remembering Sequencing in the Metric System
From shortest unit of measure to the longest:

millimeter (mm)
centimeter (cm)
decimeter (dm)
meter (m)
kilometer (km)

Remember this silly acronym: <u>M</u>y <u>C</u>at <u>D</u>rank <u>M</u>ilky <u>K</u>etchup

The **M** in **My** is for **millimeter**.
The **C** in **Cat** is for **centimeter**
The **D** in **Drank** is for **decimeter**
The **M** in **Milky** is for **meter**
The **K** in **Ketchup** is for **kilometer**

Capacity - Liquid

Milliliters - A unit of liquid measure in the metric system. (ml) is the abbreviation for milliliters. 1000 milliliters is 1 liter. Since a milliliter is often measured using an eyedropper, this prop is useful in teaching the term. Try one of these rhymes to help define!

Eye dropper, eye dropper,
How much do you hold?
Just a milliliter
Is what I've been told!

Or:
Millie had an eyedropper,
Couldn't hold a liter,
She filled it up with water,
And called it Millie Liter. (milliliter)

<u>Liter</u> - A unit of liquid measure in the metric system. A liter bottle of soda is something children are probably familiar with. Bring in the bottle and have them say this rhyme.

A liter bottle
Full of Coke
Drank so much
I thought I'd choke!

Another little rhyme to remember how to compare a liter to a pint.

**A liter of water
Is a pint and three quarter.**

Weight

Grams - The gram is a unit of mass in the metric system. It is used to measure the weight of light objects. A paper clip is about 1 gram.

**Pardon me Ma'am,
How much is a gram?
A paper clip you say,
Now you made my day!**

Kilogram – The kilogram is a unit of weight in the metric system. (kg) is the abbreviation for kilogram. "Kilo" means one thousand. Thus, there are 1000 grams in a kilogram. A math book weighs about 1 kilogram.

**"My math book is heavy," said Sam
It weighs about a kilogram.**

A rhyme comparing kilograms to pounds:

**2 ¼ pounds of jam
Weigh about a kilogram**

Fractions Can Be Fun!

The terms and words used in the study of fractions are difficult for students. They often understand how to perform a procedure but are not able to connect that skill with the linguistic term used to describe it. For example, frequently children "freeze" when asked to find the "Common Denominator." They know how to do the process, but the words confuse them and they go "blank". The purpose here is to give students some visual and memory methods to remember the term and connect it with the process of working the problem.

A fraction has two terms: the numerator and the denominator. The numerator, written above the line, tells us how many parts we are considering, while the denominator, written below the line, tells us into how many parts the whole has been divided.

Numerator – The number above the fraction bar in a fraction.

$$\frac{2}{9}$$ 2 is the numerator

Denominator – The number below the fraction bar in a fraction.

$$\frac{2}{9}$$ 9 is the denominator

Students are often unsure of the terms and where they belong. To remember which number is the numerator and which is the denominator, think

"N" for "<u>n</u>o"   <u>N</u>umerator
"D" for "<u>d</u>rugs" <u>D</u>enominator

Mixed number - A number written as a whole number and a fraction. $2\frac{1}{4}$

A mixed number is a mixture of both a fraction and a whole number. Many students will understand this concept if they can see a picture. Using a pie example often helps.

Proper Fractions - A proper fraction is a fraction whose numerator is <u>less</u> than its denominator.

$$\frac{5}{6}$$

A good method to remember the term "Proper Fraction", is by thinking that this is the best way to work with a fraction, when the numerator is smaller than the denominator, therefore it is the **proper** way for a fraction to be.

Discuss the meaning of the word "proper" (def: the best thing to do) and use it in other contexts such as, "is it <u>proper</u> to wear shoes to school?" Never assume a child understands the meaning of a word. Second language learners especially need this reinforcement.

Improper Fractions - A fraction in which the numerator is greater than or equal to the denominator.

$$\frac{7}{4} \quad \text{and} \quad \frac{6}{6} \quad \text{are Improper Fractions.}$$

Using a picture of a bigger boy standing on a board on top of a smaller boy can illustrate this definition. Explain that it isn't proper to have the larger boy on top. (Improper fraction)

Proper Fraction   **Improper Fraction**

Common Denominators – A common multiple of the denominators of two or more fractions.

When the above definition is given, the student will be more confused than before! It is actually very simple. Find the denominator, (remember "no drugs" and notice it is the number below the line). Now define the word "common" which means having something that is the same. Point out two students with something in common (such as eye color or same color shirt etc.), to illustrate the point. In this example:

$$\frac{6}{8} \text{ and } \frac{3}{8} \text{ and } \frac{7}{8}$$

The eights are what the fractions have in common and they are the denominators, therefore the eights are the common denominator.

Fractions in Lowest Terms - A fraction is in the lowest terms when the greatest common factor of the numerator and the denominator is 1.

Instruct students to associate the words "fractions in lowest terms" with the process. Explain that making fractions into the lowest terms, simply means to make the fraction numbers smaller.

1. Write $\frac{18}{24}$ as a fraction in lowest terms.

2. Find the factors of 18 and 24. Using a box is sometimes helpful and convenient. Tell the students to stop when they find 2 numbers alike.

÷	1	2	3	4
18	18	9	⑥	
24	24	12	8	⑥

3. Circle the <u>greatest</u> or largest number that both the 18 and 24 have in common, which is 6.

4. Now divide the fraction by 6. $\frac{3}{4}$ is the lowest term.

Least Common Denominator - The least common multiple of the denominators of two or more fractions. Sometimes students need some help in remembering the steps in working out the process.

Find the least common denominator for this example using memory clues.

$$\frac{1}{2} \text{ and } \frac{2}{3} \text{ and } \frac{3}{4}$$

Least Common Denominator. (L.C.D.)

L - **Look** at the denominators to see if they are the same.

$$2 \text{ and } 3 \text{ and } 4 \quad \text{are not the same.}$$

C - **Common** number. Find a common (or same) denominator for all the fractions. Find it by writing the multiples for each denominator.
Multiples of 2, 3 and 4:

$$2 \qquad 2, 4, 6, 8, 10, \boxed{12,} 14$$

$$3 \qquad 3, 6, 9, \boxed{12,} 14$$

$$4 \qquad 4, 8, \boxed{12,} 16$$

Circle the **LOWEST** multiple that is common to all the denominators.

D - **Denominator** - the least common denominator is 12.

Equivalent Fractions - Fractions that are equal in value. The "equ" in equivalent gives the clue for equal.

$$\frac{2}{4} \quad \frac{1}{2} \quad \frac{4}{8} \quad \frac{8}{16} \quad \frac{5}{10}$$

All of these fractions equal one half (1/2) and are known as equivalent fractions.

Comparing Fractions - Compare the denominators to determine if the fractions are "like fractions".   If they are, it is easy to compare to see which numerator is greater.

$$\frac{4}{8} \quad > \quad \frac{2}{8}$$

Since the 4 is greater than 2, it is the greater fraction. Just remember, larger numerator, larger fraction.

With "unlike fractions," compare the denominators.

$$\frac{4}{5} \text{ and } \frac{2}{3} \quad \text{not the same}$$

Change to like fractions by multiplying the numerator by the opposite denominator. Multiply 4/5 by 3/3 and multiply 2/3 by 5/5. Since 3/3 and 5/5 are equal to 1, the value does not change.

$$\frac{4}{5} \diagdown \diagdown \frac{2}{3} \qquad \frac{4}{5} \times \frac{3}{3} = \frac{12}{15} \qquad \frac{2}{3} \times \frac{5}{5} = \frac{10}{15}$$

15 is the common denominator. Now the comparison is easy. They are "like fractions."

$$\frac{12}{15} \quad > \quad \frac{10}{15}$$

Inverting Fractions - To put the denominator in the numerator's place and to put the numerator in the denominator's place. Have the students look up the meaning for invert in the dictionary; to turn upside down or reverse the order. Discuss other things that can be inverted such as an object turned upside down. Apply this reversal idea to inverting fractions.

$$\frac{3}{4} \quad \text{inverted would be} \quad \frac{4}{3}$$

Other Fraction Ideas to Explore

Fractions can be incorporated into art projects. Cut out different shapes on colored paper by folding into equal parts. Label the sections and write the fractions. Talk about fractions as being a part of the whole. Hang these shapes from a piece of string spanning an area or make individual mobiles.

Another activity is to make a fraction book. Students draw and make up fraction problems on each page. They write the answer to the problem on the back of the page under a little flap. This way they can share the book with other students and everyone can have fun answering the problems.

What we learn with pleasure
We never forget.
Alfred Mercier

Deciphering Decimals

Understanding Decimals

In order to introduce decimals to children, using the following method, they need to have had some previous experience with fractions (in particular, tenths.) Visual children respond to this method because they can "see" what it means.

1) Draw a rectangle on the board and split it into ten sections. Ask a child how we can label each section of the rectangle (i.e. 1/10). Write 1/10 in each section...

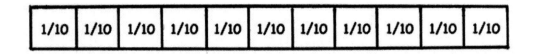

2) Color some of the rectangles,

3) Ask the children what fraction of the rectangle has been colored (i.e. 1/10 + 1/10 + 1/10 = 3/10).

4) Explain that 3/10 can be written in another way, 0.3 (no units and three tenths). The dot in between the 0 and the 3 is called the DECIMAL POINT and is used to separate the units from the tenths. By writing in the 0 before the decimal point, reminds us that the whole number is less than one.

Use this Place Value Chart to help students understand how decimals are used. The child has been taught place value being: Hundreds, Tens, Ones. Now a decimal is added and to the right of the decimal is something called the "tenths" place and next to it on the right, is the "hundredths" place, then the "thousandths" place. If this concept can be illustrated visually it is easier to understand. Use this type of chart and call out numbers with decimals, having the students fill it in.

Hundreds Tens Ones Decimal Tenths Hundredths Thousandths

_____

_____

_____

Since students are familiar with hundreds, tens and ones place, the only new information will be the decimal, tenths, hundredths and thousandths.

It is fun to play games where students say the places aloud so they can hear themselves making the differentiation in the words and understanding the placement. Learning takes place when the child hears himself or herself actually say the words. Remember, one of the keys to memorization is repetition ALOUD! Try this activity:

Put the chart above on an overhead and write in numbers using the decimal. Have the students work in groups and determine how to read the number. Each group gets a chance to read the numbers in unison. Or ask the value for an individual number. This should not be a competition game but an activity where each student can participate and feel confident.

When adding or subtracting decimals, use graph paper and allow a separate square for the decimal. Call out numbers. Students place them in the correct box. Graph paper makes it easier to keep the numbers lined up correctly.

Comparing and Ordering Decimals
Again use the graph paper. To compare decimals, follow these steps.
1. Line up the decimal points

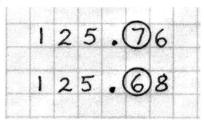

2. Start at the left. Compare numbers in each column to see if they are the same or different.

3. The first greater digit is the greater decimal.
125.76 > 125.68

Rounding Decimals

Rounding decimals can be very confusing to many children. If children have an easily remembered system, they feel more confident. These steps make it simple.

Round this decimal, 1.152 to the nearest tenth.

1. Find the rounding place and underline it.   1 . <u>1</u> 5 2
2. Look at the digit to the right.   1 . <u>1</u> 5 2

If it is less than 5, leave the underlined digit unchanged.

If it is 5 or more, increase the underlined digit by one.   1 . 2

Get rid of all the other digits to the right of it.

Say this little rhyme to remember the procedure.
Underline the rounding place and look to the right.
If its under 5, it sits tight.
5 or over means, underlined goes higher.
Forget the other numbers, they can take a flyer.

Geometry - Now This is Fun!

Usually visual learners do well with geometry because they can see and work with the figures on paper. Geometry can be a lot of fun and this book will be stressing the vocabulary of geometry. Students frequently struggle with the meaning of mathematical words.

Using the Latin base for a word is helpful. For example, the word "geometry" can be broken down to "geo" meaning earth and "metry" meaning to measure. This is the dictionary definition of the word: "*The mathematics of the properties, measurement, and relationships of points, lines, angles, surfaces, and solids.*" In other words, measuring things pertaining to the earth. Teaching geometric terms is an excellent time to introduce the base word meaning and tie it into a vocabulary lesson.

Circle- A round enclosed figure. All students are aware of the circle but the words for measuring parts of the circle are often confusing.

Semicircle - A half circle. Semi means half or part of. Students need to draw the shapes and label them in order to have the information retained in their brain.

Circumference - The line bounding a circle. A simple memory tip for this word is to instruct the student to draw a large circle and write the word all around the edge. Placing dashes between the syllables is helpful for pronunciation. Point out that "cir" is said the same as in <u>cir</u>cle.

Diameter - A line segment that passes through the center of the circle and has both endpoints on the circle. Again draw the circle and place the diameter through the middle and make it into a capital "D". The Greek for "dia" is "through" or "across" and "meter" means measure. Therefore, the word diameter means measuring across the circle.

Radius - A line segment with one end point on the circle and the other end point at the center. Since the Latin meaning for the word is ray or the spoke of a wheel, it is easy to visualize radius as a spoke coming from the center of the wheel.

Use this rhyme and write the words accordingly. <u>Radius</u> **short, <u>d i a m e t e r</u> long, remember this, and you'll never go wrong!**
Read *Sir Cumference and the First Round Table*. This cleverly written storybook provides an association method to remember these terms. (See Product Resources)

Chord - A chord is a line segment with both endpoints on the circle. The diameter is the longest chord on a circle.

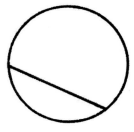

---

*Memory Tip: Draw and label
to learn the term!*

Lines

Understanding the terminology of lines is vital for students. By using pictures, the terms become much easier to remember.

Point - A point shows an exact location in space. It is often named by using a capital letter. Students usually understand the meaning of point.

. **A**

Line - A geometric figure formed by a point moving along a fixed direction and the reverse direction. This is best demonstrated by having students draw a straight line with a ruler continuing off their paper on both sides. Talk about how a line goes on forever. By adding arrows to each end, it shows that the line goes on into infinity.

Line Segment - A part of a line. It has two endpoints. "Seg" means "to cut" in Latin. By using the word "segment" as a vocabulary word while teaching this concept, it makes the understanding easier. Instruct students to draw a line, and add end points to any part of it, illustrating the idea of a segment of a line.

Ray - A ray is a part of a line. It has one endpoint and goes on and on in one direction. The best visual for a ray is by drawing the sun and rays coming out from it. They are already familiar with the term "ray of sun" and by calling their attention to the end point (at the sun's center), they have the definition. Discuss how a ray of sun can go on and on in space and therefore it is necessary to show the arrow at the end of the ray.

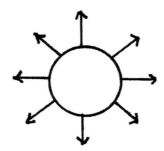

Plane - A plane is a flat surface that extends in all directions without end. It has no thickness.

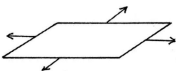

When students hear the word "plane" they naturally think of an airplane. Have fun with the word and draw airplanes with wings that extend on and on. Talk about the wings as being a plane.

Intersecting - Students are usually familiar with the term "intersection" as the place where two streets cross. By drawing streets crossing and labeling the intersection, it becomes easy to remember.

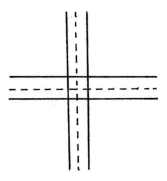

Parallel - Lines in the same plane that are equal distance apart and never intersect. An easy way to remember this meaning is to write the word and color the straight L's another color showing parallel lines.

parallel

```
Memory Tip:
Challenge students to create
their own ways to remember
math words!
```

Perpendicular - Lines that intersect and/or form right angles. Write perpendicular emphasizing the word PEN. Per**PEN**dicular

Telling a silly little limerick along with a picture depicting the pen with <u>perpendicular</u> lines, will help students remember the meaning. Remember, the sillier something is, the easier it is to retain.

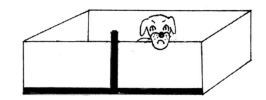

There once was a fellow named Per
Whose dog, always said "Grrrrr"
Per built him a pen
And put the dog in
And called it perpendicular.

Horizontal - Parallel to or in the plane of the horizon. Point out the word horizon in **horizon**tal. Discuss the meaning of horizon. Write the word spreading out the letters to emphasize the horizontal line.

h   o   r   i   z   o   n   t   a   l

Vertical - Being or situated at right angles to the horizon; upright. Discuss how "vertical" and "horizontal" are perpendicular to each other. This word can be written from the bottom of the paper (the horizontal line) up. By doing an activity a little differently, it is easier to remember.

l
a
c
i
t
r
e
v

Tessellation - A tessellation is an arrangement of polygonal regions covering the plane without overlapping or leaving any gaps. In simpler terms, a tessellation is a design that repeats over and over by **reflection** (flip), **rotation** (turn) or **translation** (slide). The only way to really understand the meaning of tessellation, is by doing fun art projects using the various terms. There are a lot of free patterns and instructions available on the internet. Encourage students to say the words "tessellation, reflection, rotation and translation" aloud as they apply them to their art projects.

Reflection - To remember the meaning of **reflection,** write the word and then challenge the students to write it as if it were being reflected or flipped over.

Rotation - This is easy to remember since children are familiar with the earth rotating or turning. Demonstrate the word by rotating an object.

Translation - This term is a little more challenging to remember. By noticing the "sl" in the word tranSlation, children can make an association with the word "slide" which is the definition. By sliding pieces of paper around in a tessellation, the term becomes familiar.

This is a great time to incorporate these terms into a paper quilt art project. Locate a wallpaper sample book and cut small patterns into 3" x 3" squares. Students make up repeating quilt designs and glue the pieces onto a 9" or 12"square piece of construction paper. After students complete individual squares, tape them together to form a large classroom quilt. Dale Seymour Publications has books on the subject. Good historical literature is *Eight Hands Around* by Ann Whitford Paul and *The Keeping Quilt* by Patricia Polacco. M.C. Escher designs are a good source too.

Memory Tip:
Memory is enhanced when a student
explains or "teaches" the problem solution
to another person.

Polygons

Polygon - A many sided closed figure with corners. "Poly" means many. Think of looking down at the top of a cage for Polly the Parrot with many, many sides all connected with lines. Have the students draw many possible shapes for the bird's eye view of Polly's cage.

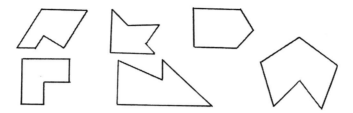

To understand polygons, it is necessary to draw and label all of the figures shown below. The pictures can be assembled into a Polygon Book. Use color as it helps children remember information.

The figure below is not a polygon, since it is not a closed figure.

The figure below is not a polygon, since it is not made of line segments.

The figure below is not a polygon, since its sides do not intersect in exactly two places each.

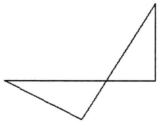

Quadrilateral - A polygon with four sides and four angles. Explain the definition of "quad" as meaning four. Use the word "quad" as much as possible by having 4 students forming a quad. Explain that "lateral" means side. In football a lateral pass is to the side. Use the word in a game where you pass the ball laterally.

Use new vocabulary words in every day situations. Don't forget memorization takes place for audio learners when they say the words aloud and explain it to others. The following shapes are all quadrilaterals but they also have more definitive names.

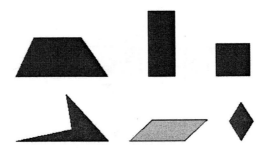

Square - A four-sided polygon having equal-length sides meeting at right angles. The sum of the angles of a square is 360 degrees.

Rectangle - A four-sided polygon having all right angles. The sum of the angles of a rectangle is 360 degrees. A rectangle can also be explained as a parallelogram with 4 square corners (or 4 right angles). The Latin word, "recti" means straight or right. The word "right" is similar to "recti", they both begin with "r" and have a "t". Discuss the 4 right angles and make the comparison with the Latin word. Point out that a square can also be considered a rectangle. Challenge students to discover the difference.

Memory Tip:
Kinesthetic learners need to touch the shapes.
Provide plastic pattern blocks for them to manipulate.

Trapezoid - A quadrilateral with exactly one pair of opposite sides parallel. To associate the word "trapezoid" with the shape can be accomplished by drawing a picture after hearing this silly story. Students can draw their own ezoid space figure inside a trapezoid and write the story.

An "ezoid," an outer space being, arrived in his space ship "The Trapezoid". But as he tried to get out, the door wouldn't open and he realized he was trapped!

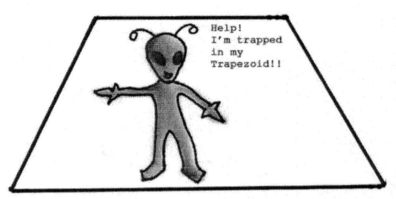

Parallelogram - A quadrilateral with opposite sides parallel and congruent. Before the student can grasp the meaning of this definition, he/she will need to know the meaning of parallel and congruent. Remember, notice the parallel "L's" in the word. Color the "L's" a bright color.

para l l el

Congruent - Figures that have the same size and shape. Since this word is used in the definition of parallelogram, this is a good time to provide a memory tip for the meaning of congruent. Explain that congruent figures like twins can be in different positions (flipped over) yet they are still congruent.

Congruent, congruent are twins, you know.
Their size and their shape are the same as they grow.

Once these terms are understood, the next step is to apply them to the word, "parallelogram." Drawing parallelograms and labeling them helps to make the connection. Instruct the students to draw a quadrilateral (4 sided) shape with opposite sides parallel (same direction) and congruent (same length). Explore many shapes for parallelograms.

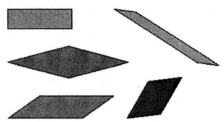

To remember the definition of a parallelogram, notice that the word, **parallel** has three "L's" in it and three conditions.
1. Must be a quadrilateral.
2. Opposite sides must be parallel.
3. Opposite sides must be congruent.

Similar - Similar figures have the same shape but they may or may not have the same size.

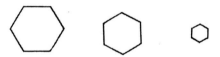

Rhombus - A parallelogram with all sides congruent.
Since students now understand the meaning of parallelogram and congruent, the definition for rhombus is easier. The trick here is making a connection between the shape and the name, rhombus. Again, associations and drawing seem to be the key. Notice the word "bus" in "rhombus". Draw a bus called the "Rhombus" by making all sides congruent and parallel. Add some wheels and label it the "Rhombus."

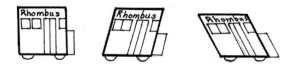

Triangle - A figure with 3 sides and 3 corners. The sum of the angles of a triangle is 180 degrees.

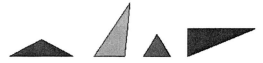

"Tri" means three in Latin. This is a good time to discover other words with "tri" at the beginning of the word.

tricycle with three wheels
triceratops has three horns
triathlon - a contest with three endurance events
trilingual - using three languages
triad - a group of three things, persons, ideas or a musical chord of three tones.

Equilateral Triangle - All sides are congruent (the same or equal). The angles of an equilateral triangle all measure 60 degrees.
Equi = equal Lateral = sides

Isosceles Triangle - Has two congruent or same sides.
Sing this to the tune of "Oh Christmas Tree":

Oh isosceles, oh isosceles
Two angles have
Equal degrees

Oh isosceles, oh isosceles
You look just like
A Christmas tree

Scalene Triangle - Has no congruent sides. Each side is a different length. This word can be easily remembered because it sounds like "scaling" and students are familiar with "hikers scaling mountains." The scalene triangle has no congruent sides, same as a mountain. Now there is a connection. Draw mountains made of scalene triangles and show a hiker scaling it. Label the drawing.

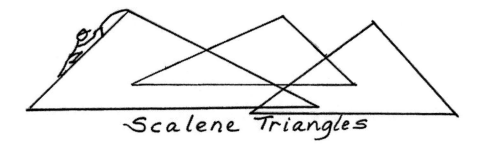

Right Triangle - Has one right angle of 90 degrees.

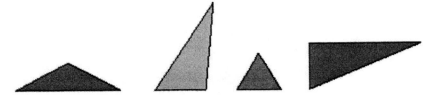

Challenge students to find which triangles are Right Triangles. Hint: look for lines that are perpendicular. Use a protractor to check for 90 degrees.

Pentagon - A figure with 5 sides and 5 corners. The sum of the angles of a pentagon is 540 degrees.

"Penta" means five. There is a building in Washington, D.C. called the Pentagon and it has 5 sides. Have students draw the floor plan of the five-sided building and label it "pentagon."

A regular pentagon

An irregular pentagon

Memory Tip: To remember that "penta" means 5, think about your 5 fingers holding your pen.

Hexagon - A figure with 6 sides and 6 corners. The sum of the angles of a hexagon is 720 degrees. "Hexa" means six.

A regular hexagon

An irregular hexagon

> *Memory Tip:*
> *The word si<u>x</u> has an <u>X</u> in it*
> *and so does he<u>x</u>agon.*
> *Just remember the X.*

Octagon - A figure with 8 sides and 8 corners. The sum of the angles of an octagon is 1080 degrees. "Octo" means eight. Explore other words that begin with "octo." Discuss October and how it was the eighth month before the Roman calendar was changed in 1582.

Students can draw an octopus with eight legs, then draw an octagon with eight sides and corners.

Angles - Two rays with a common end point.
Practice drawing angles in different configurations.

Right Angle - An angle measuring 90 degrees.
This is a good introduction into learning about degrees; the unit for measuring angles. By using a protractor, it is easy to visualize angle measurement.

Acute Angle - An angle that measures less than 90 degrees.
Remembering the definition of the word "acute" can be tied into a vocabulary lesson. "Acute" means critical, severe or having a sharp point. An acute angle is much sharper and looks more severe than a right angle. Use those protractors again to check!

Obtuse Angle - An angle that measures more than 90 degrees.
The word "obtuse" provides another opportunity to study the meaning of words. Pick a student to look up the word in the Dictionary. Obtuse means the opposite of acute - not sharp or pointed. The word can be illustrated by drawing an obtuse angle and making it into a reclining chair, something open and relaxed.

Vertex - The point of intersection of two angles.

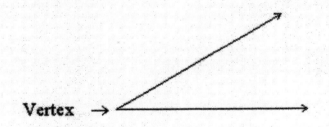

Remember the meaning by saying this little verse:

A vertex is a point
Where angles form a joint

Line of Symmetry - Divides a figure into two congruent parts.
This term can be more easily remembered by doing art projects incorporating lines of symmetry and having students use the term in conversation. Teachers can point out objects having lines of symmetry. Art projects include butterflies, hearts, paper dolls, etc.

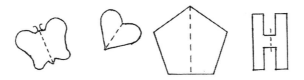

Memory Tip:
Symmetry sounds a little like "same"
and means the same on each side.
Sym and Same, like a little bee
Help you remember symmetry.

All of these terms can be more easily remembered by doing art projects incorporating the figures. An excellent book with easy to make geometric shape projects, is *Math for Fun, Exploring Shapes* by Andrew King. (See Product Resources for more information.)

The role that memory training plays in
overcoming learning disabilities,
is grossly underestimated.
D. Yates

Geometry We Can Touch

Sphere - A space figure shaped like a round ball.

Our world is a <u>sphere</u> with atmo<u>sphere</u>! Draw it.

Cube - A space figure with 6 square faces.

A cube is easy, just think of an ice cube!! Draw it and count the 6 sides.

Rectangular prism - A space figure whose faces are all rectangles.
Since students know what a rectangle is, the other word to learn is prism. Prism sounds a little like "prison" and a prison cell has enclosed space and could be a rectangular shape or a triangular shape.

Make a drawing of a rectangular prism that looks like a prison.

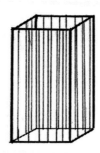

Triangular Prism - A space figure whose base is a triangle with rectangular sides.

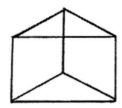

Pyramid - A space figure whose base is a polygon and whose faces are triangles, meeting at one point at the top or vertex. Point out the difference in the base shape, between a triangular prism and a pyramid. Children are usually familiar with the Great Pyramids of Egypt, so this is a good time to show pictures and determine if they are square pyramids, rectangular pyramids or triangular pyramids.

 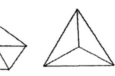

Square   Rectangular   Triangular

When the students draw these pyramids, they will be surprised by the optical illusions that are created!

Cone - A space figure with a circular base with rounded sides meeting at a point. Too easy!

Draw an ice cream cone!

Cylinder - A space figure with 2 bases that are the same size.
A cylinder is another name for a can and a can is a cylinder. The word "silly" comes to mind with the word "cylinder".

Draw a "silly cylinder!"

Face - A flat surface of a space figure.
Make drawings of different figures with smiley faces on the face surface.

Edge - The segment where two faces of a space figure meet. Draw geometric shapes and label the edges.

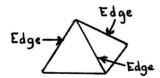

Corner - The position at which two lines, surfaces, or edges meet and form an angle. Corners are easy!

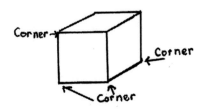

For all of these space figures, remember that visual learners need to draw and label, kinesthetic learners need to touch, and audio learners need to explain it to everyone

---

Memory Tip:
Our brains are meaning-making machines, searching for matches to previous experiences.

Those Roaming Roman Numerals

Counting in Roman Numerals.

One	I	Eleven	XI	Thirty	XXX
Two	II	Twelve	XII	Forty	XL
Three	III	Thirteen	XIII	Fifty	L
Four	IV	Fourteen	XIV	Sixty	LX
Five	V	Fifteen	XV	Seventy	LXX
Six	VI	Sixteen	XVI	Eighty	LXXX
Seven	VII	Seventeen	XVII	Ninety	XC
Eight	VIII	Eighteen	XVIII	One Hundred	C
Nine	IX	Nineteen	XIX	Five Hundred	D
Ten	X	Twenty	XX	One Thousand	M

To remember the letter designations in order for one, five, ten, fifty, hundred, five hundred and thousand, use the letter symbol and make up a silly sentence. The more ridiculous the acronym, the better chance of remembering it.

I =	One		I = I
V =	Five		V = View
X =	Ten		X = X-rays
L =	Fifty		L = Like
C =	Hundred		C = Cows
D =	Five-hundred		D = Drink
M =	Thousand		M = Milk

<u>I</u> <u>V</u>iew <u>X</u>-rays <u>L</u>ike <u>C</u>ows <u>D</u>rink <u>M</u>ilk.

How about using this memory technique for audio learners to remember L, C, D, M? Just remember the world famous Vietnamese cow,

Elsie Diem
(Elsie L,C, and Diem D, M.)

Or try these visual memory methods:

  I = One (This is no problem.)

  V = Five (Remember the V in five.)

  X = Ten (X is made up of 2 V's, with one upside down on the bottom.)

L = 50 (A 50 yr. old leaping leprechaun, which ties the 50 to "L" words.)

C = 100 (Use the "C" in cents and associate it with 100 cents.)
"C" also stands for "century" which is 100 years.

D = 500 (Instead of 100 Dalmatians, think of 5 times as many, 500 Dotted Dalmatians.)

M = 1000 (Students often think M stands for million, by writing the word thousand around the M, it helps to clarify the error.)

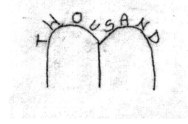

Algebra Basics - So Easy to Remember!

Equation - Facts that are equal to each other on both sides of the = symbol.

Example.: 3 + 4 - 2 = 6 + 3 - 4

7 - 2 = 9 - 4

5 = 5

The easiest way to teach the meaning of an equation is by showing a balance scale. There are products available that are weighted and provide the visual concept necessary for many learners.

To remember the procedural order of operations
Use the first letter in each word of the acronym to remember the procedure.

Please   Excuse   My   Dear   Aunt Sally
Parentheses, Exponents, Multiply, Divide, Add, Subtract

Multiplying Two Binomials

F O I L

This cue word stands for the steps in multiplying two binomials:

multiply the <u>First</u> terms (F)

multiply the <u>Outer</u> terms (O)

multiply the <u>Inner</u> (O) terms

multiply the <u>Last</u> terms (L)

Example: For the problem of (x + 3)(x + 2) =

F: (x + 3)(x + 2) Multiply the First symbols inside each bracket.

x times x = x squared.

O: (x + 3)(x + 2) Multiply the Outer symbols inside each bracket.

x times 2 = 2x

I: (x + 3)(x + 2) Multiply the Inner symbols inside each bracket.

3 times x = 3x

L: (x + 3)(x + 2) Multiply the Last symbols inside each bracket.

3 times 2 = 6

Properties

Commutative property of addition $a + b = b + a$
Commutative property of multiplication $ab = ba$
The Commutative Property, in general, states that changing the ORDER of two numbers either being added or multiplied, does NOT change the value of it. The two sides are called equivalent expressions because they look different but have the same value.

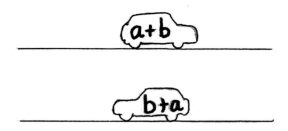

Commutative sounds like commute. To commute or travel somewhere you go one way and come back the same way. Think of a road with "a" driving one way and "b" as the passenger. They drive back with "b" driving and "a" as the passenger.

Associative property of addition $(a + b) + c = a + (b + c)$
Associative property of multiplication $(ab) c = a (bc)$
The Associative property, in general, states that changing the GROUPING of numbers that are either being added or multiplied does NOT change the value of it. The two sides are equivalent to each other.

Associative sounds like associating in a group. No matter what groups are formed, their value remains the same.

$$(a + b) + c = a + (b + c)$$

Substitute the letters with number values and try it out. $a = 4$, $b = 6$, $c = 3$

Distributive property   a (b + c) = ab + ac

When you have a term being multiplied times two or more terms that are being added (or subtracted) in a parenthesis, multiply the outside term times EVERY term on the inside.

To distribute means to pass around. Think of the brackets as an enclosure with b + c inside. "a" comes up and wants to hookup with "b" but that leaves "c" all alone, so "a" hooks-up with "c" too. "a" is being distributed to each symbol inside.

$$a(b+c) \;=\; ab + ac$$

Just Remember....

We retain 10 percent of what we read;
20 percent of what we hear;
30 percent of what we see;
50 percent of what we hear and see;
70 percent of what we say;
90 percent of what we say and do!

Afterword.....

This book is like a growing tree. It is designed to grow through your suggestions and tried methods. No one can possibly know the many mnemonic and visual ideas used to teach children. I challenge you to be a part of this book. There will be revisions as it grows, and credit will be acknowledged for your submissions, if you so desire. Thank you!

Please send your ideas to
Donnalyn Yates
24 Nuevo
Irvine, CA 92612
888-854-9400
E-Mail: donnalyn@memoryjoggers.com

Other Books and Products by the Author

Thought for the Day Book- Classroom Edition by Donnalyn Yates
Character building writing prompts that are appealing to children of all ages. 365 journal writing prompts for each day of the year.

Memory Joggers Multiplication/Div. Learning Systems by Donnalyn Yates
Resource for memorizing mult./div. facts 0 – 9.
66 page Activity Book for mult./div.
Memorizing system for 10, 11, 12 facts.

Memory Joggers Addition/Subtraction Learning Systems by Donnalyn Yates
Resource for memorizing add/sub.facts.
67 page Activity Book for add/sub.
CD of all rhymes

Contact Memory Joggers:
24 Nuevo – Irvine, CA 92612
888-854-9400
www.memoryjoggers.com

Product Resources

The Crayon Counting Book by Pam Munoz Ryan
    Charlesbridge Publishing

Eight Hands Around by Ann Whitford Paul.
    Historical quilt book displaying quilt patterns in Colonial times.

The Keeping Quilt by Patricia Polacco.
    Literature book about a quilt passed on through the generations.

Introduction to Tessellations by Dale Seymour and Jill Britton

Math for Fun - Exploring Shapes by Andrew King
    This book is an excellent resource for teaching geometric shapes. The
    projects are easy to do and the book is colorfully illustrated.
    Copper Beech Books (an imprint of The Millbrook Press)
    2 Old New Milford Road
    Brookfield, Connecticut 06804

Memory Joggers Learning Systems by Donnalyn Yates
    Memory method resource for learning systems mentioned in this book.
    Multiplication/Division & Addition/Subtraction Learning Systems.
    Memory Joggers
    24 Nuevo
    Irvine, CA 92612
    www.memoryjoggers.com
    888-854-9400

Odd Todd and Even Steven by Kathryn Cristaldi.
    Published by Scholastic, Inc.

Read It! Draw It! Solve It! by Elizabeth D. Miller
    A good resource for teaching children how to visualize word problems.
    Available for grades 1, 2, 3, 4 and 5.
    Dale Seymour Publications

Sir Cumference and the First Round Table, A Math Adventure
> By Cindy Neuschwander
> Scholastic Inc.,
> New York

Sir Cumference and the Dragon of Pi
> By Cindy Neuschwander
> Scholastic Inc.,
> New York

Appendix Section

Counting Rhymes to Ten

Name...

Appendix A

Run, **One**!

Run for fun!

Can't you see,

You're number 1

Write the number 1. Circle the best 1.

Two, two,

Shoes for you

Count them again

1, 2

Write the number 2. Circle the best 2.

2

Three, Three, Three
What do you see?
Three little birdies
In the tree.

1, 2, **3**

Write the number 3. Circle the best 3.

Four, four, four,

Four balls bouncing

On the floor.

1, 2, 3, **4**

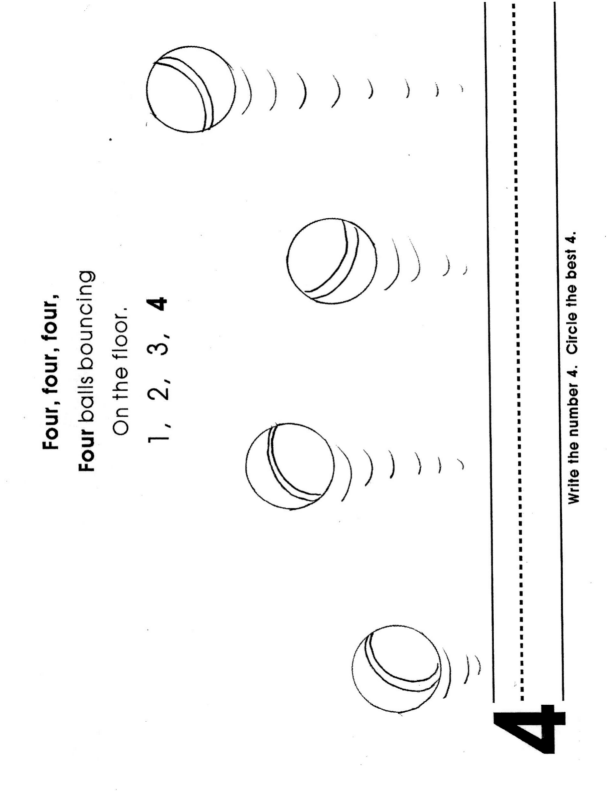

Write the number 4. Circle the best 4.

Five, five,

Take a dive

See **five** divers

Deep-sea dive!

1, 2, 3, 4, **5**

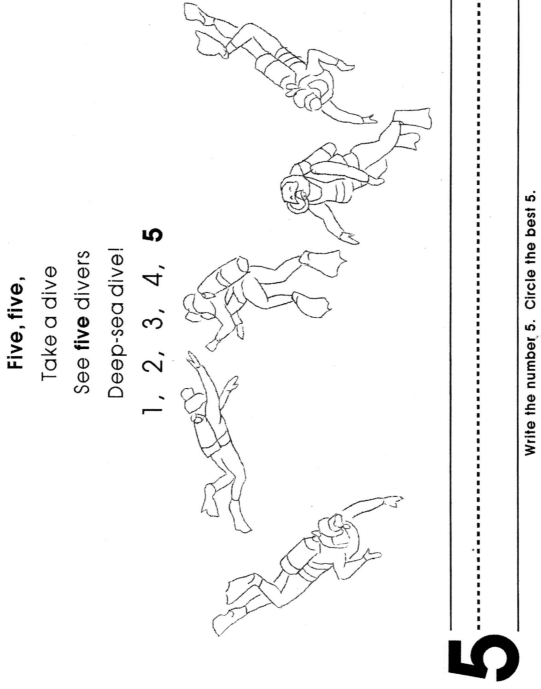

Write the number 5.   Circle the best 5.

5

Six chicks

Do some tricks

How many chicks?

1, 2, 3, 4, 5, **6**

Write the number 6. Circle the best 6.

Seven, seven!

We count to **seven!**

1, 2, 3, 4, 5, 6, 7

Write the number 7. Circle the best 7.

7

Eight, Eight!

Can't be late

To eat eight cookies

Off the plate!

1, 2, 3, 4, 5, 6, 7, 8

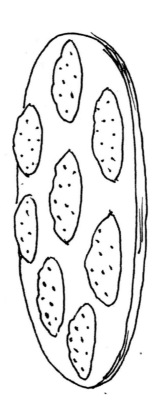

Write the number 8. Circle the best 8.

Nine, nine,
Valentines
Some are yours
Some are mine!

1, 2, 3, 4, 5, 6, 7, 8, **9**

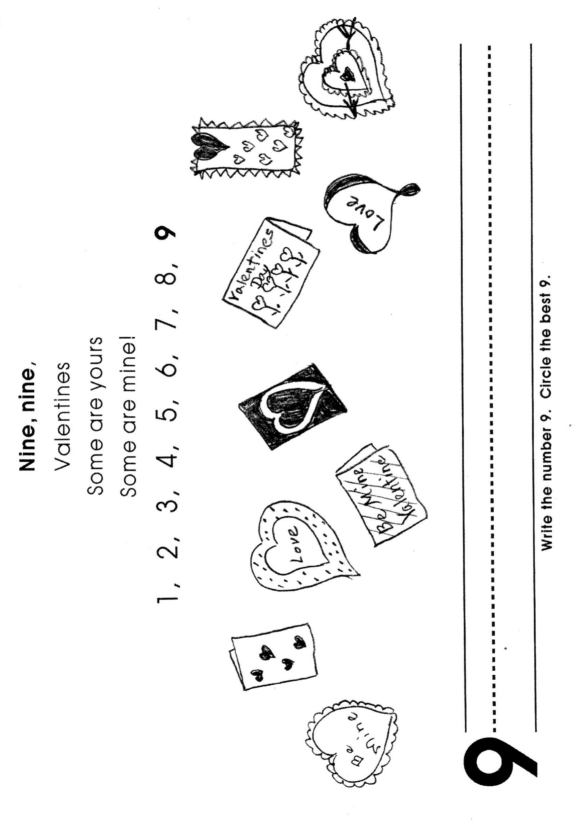

Write the number 9. Circle the best 9.

Ten, ten!

Mother hen

Layed ten eggs

In her pen!

1, 2, 3, 4, 5, 6, 7, 8, 9, **10**

10

Write the number 10. Circle the best 10.

Counting Rhymes to Twenty

Name...

Appendix B

1, 2, buckle my shoe

3, 4, close the door

5, 6, pick up sticks

Appendix B

7, 8, lay them straight

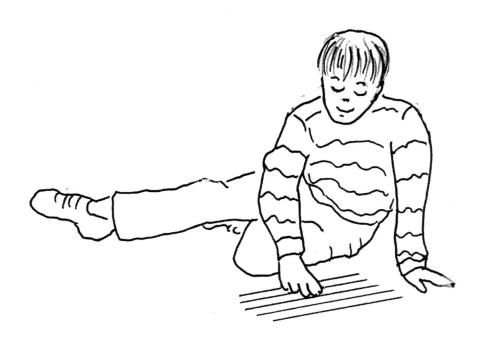

Appendix B

9, 10, a big fat hen

11, 12, eggs on a shelf

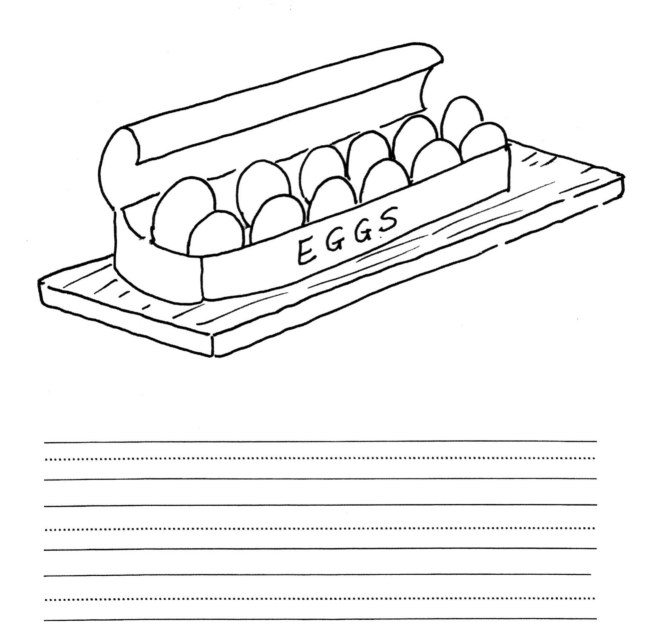

13, 14, fruit we're sorting

15, 16, cake is mixing

17, 18, dinner's waiting

19, 20, we have plenty

....

....

....

Appendix B

My Days of the Week Book

Name...

Sunday learn the Golden Rule

Golden Rule

Treat others nicely

because...

You would want them

to treat you nicely.

Monday off we go to school.

Tuesday is a day to add.

$2 + 3 = 5$

$5 + 4 = 9$

$2 + 4 = 6$

$5 + 5 = 10$

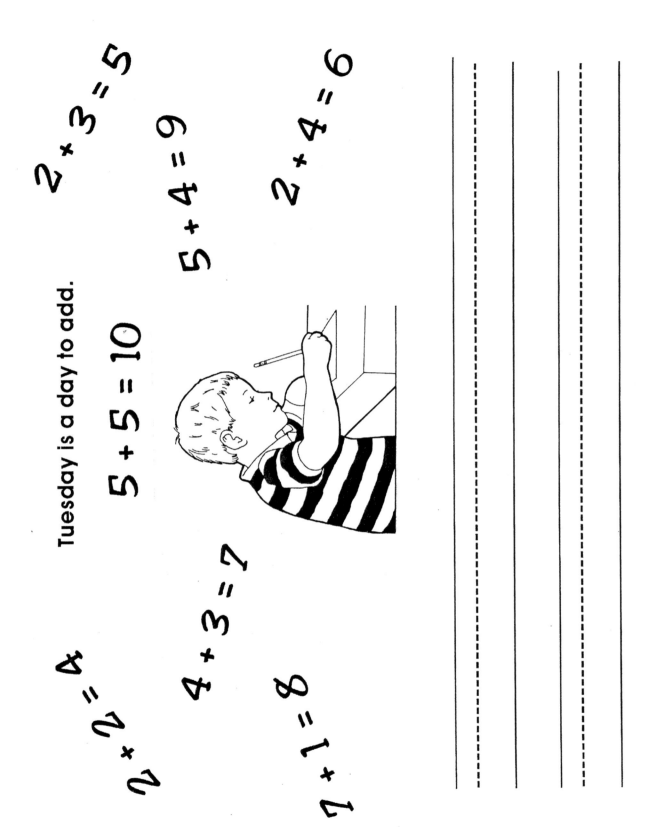

$2 + 2 = 4$

$4 + 3 = 7$

$7 + 1 = 8$

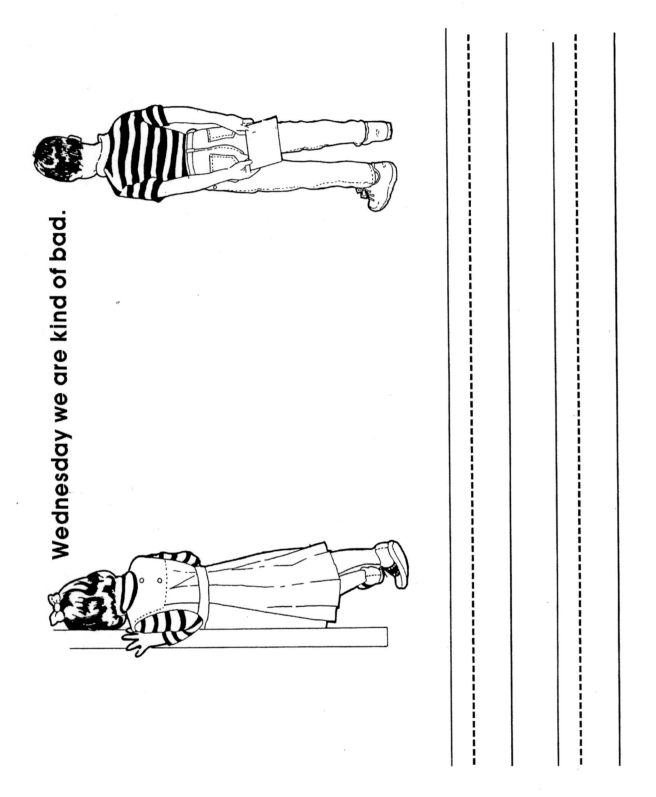

Wednesday we are kind of bad.

Thursday teacher gives a test.

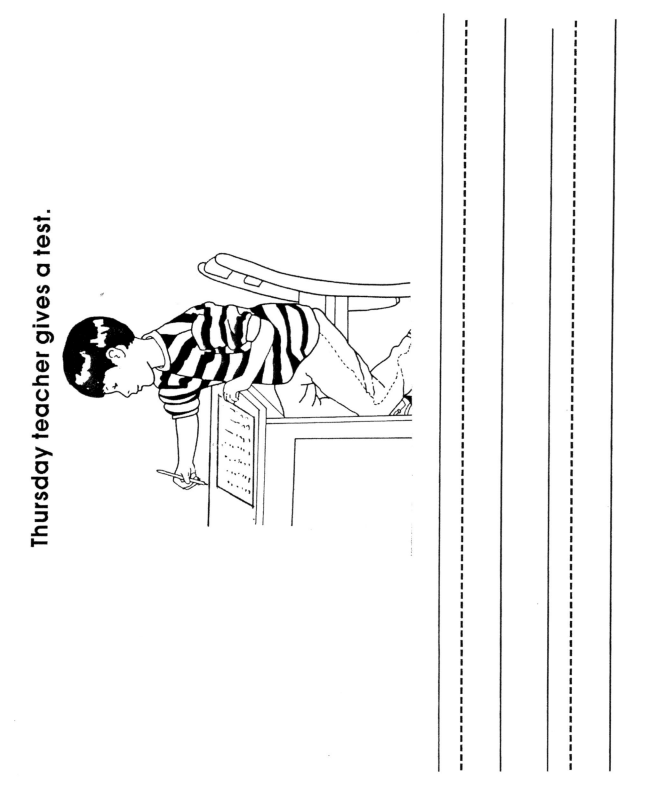

Friday we will do our best.

Saturday is here for play.

Now you know the seven days.

SUNDAY	MONDAY	TUESDAY	WEDNESDAY	THURSDAY	FRIDAY	SATURDAY
		1	2	3	4	5
6	7	8	9	10	11	12
13	14	15	16	17	18	19
20	21	22	23	24	25	26
27	28	29	30			

Month of _____

SUNDAY	MONDAY	TUESDAY	WEDNESDAY	THURSDAY	FRIDAY	SATURDAY

Appendix D

Clock Pattern

1. Cut out the clock face.
2. Glue it to a paper plate, keeping it in the center.
3. Make a small hole in the center with a paper clip.
4. Cut out the clock hands. Notice that the hour hand is shorter than the minute hand. Make small holes in the hands.
5. Attach the hands with a brad, pushing the brad through the center hole.
6. Set the clock for the current time.

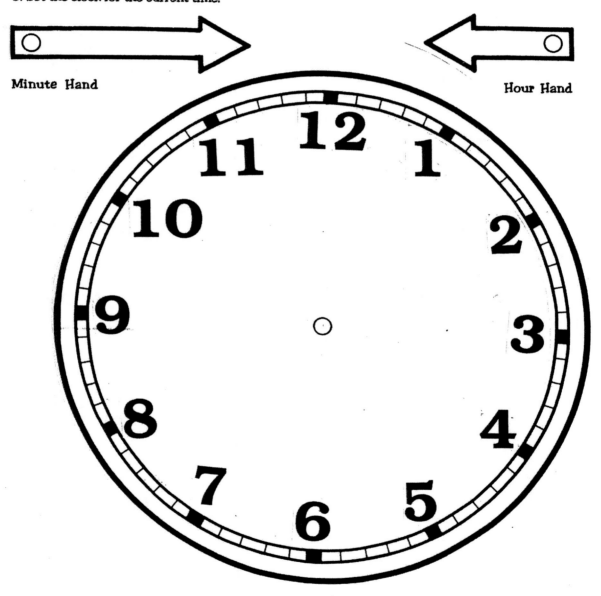

Minute Hand

Hour Hand

Appendix E

JOB APPLICATION

Name_____ Date_____

Street Address_____

City_____ State_____ Zip_____

Which job are you applying for?_____

What kind of experience do you have for doing this job?_____

_____

Why do you think you would be good at this job?

_____

Reference (another student can put their name down as a reference for you)

_____   Sign your name_____

****

JOB APPLICATION

Name_____ Date_____

Street Address_____

City_____ State_____ Zip_____

Which job are you applying for?

_____

What kind of experience do you have for doing this job?

_____

Why do you think you would be good at this job?

_____

Reference (another student can put their name down as a reference for you)

_____   Sign your name_____

Appendix F

Help Wanted

<u>Accountants</u> - Need 2 accountants. Job includes keeping track of daily attendance by marking 5 cents every day for every student who is here. On Friday, the 2 accountants will total the money earned and pay all students. Must be good at math and keeping track of money. Pay is 40 cents per week for each accountant. Apply by filling out a job application and returning it to the teacher.

<u>Homework Checker</u> - Every Friday, this person will check to see if all the class turned in their homework. This applicant must be good at reading names and keeping a chart accurately. Pay is 25 cents per week. Apply by filling out a job application and returning it to the teacher.

<u>Custodian</u> - This person will check the floor prior to the class leaving for lunch and again at the end of the day. The custodian will inform students if there is trash near their desk. Applicant must be able to tell students to clean up, using a nice voice. The custodian must be a responsible individual and remembers to do their job without being told. Pay is 30 cents per week. Apply by filling out a job application and returning it to the teacher.

Appendix G

Help Wanted

<u>Back Pack Organizer</u> - This person will check the back pack storage area every morning to see if the area is neat and organized. The person will inform anyone who did not place their back pack in the designated spot to do so. Applicant must be kind yet get the job done. Pay is 25 cents per week. Apply by filling out a job application and returning it to the teacher.

<u>Messenger</u> - This individual will be "on call" whenever the teacher needs an errand run. Must be good and hard workers in order to not get behind in class work. Dependability is crucial. Pay is 25 cents per week. Apply by filling out a job application and returning it to the teacher.

<u>Book Shelf Organizer</u> - This person will check the bookshelves daily at the end of the day to see if the books are orderly. If not, they will straighten the books neatly. Applicant must be a neat and organized person. Pay is 30 cents per week. Apply by filling out a job application and turning it in to the teacher.